Table of Contents

Crash

Shit!.......my knee hurt. A bit of blood but not too much. A lot of mud.

I tried to get back on the bike and pedal but quickly realised it wasn't going to happen. "What the hell do I do now?" Looking about, I saw a farm down at the end of the muddy track and I decided I needed to get down there. I picked up the bike (not leaving that behind!) and then, leaning heavily on the handlebars, start hopping down the track. Blood was now streaming down my leg. Coming to the realisation I needed to get to a hospital, I optimistically started wondering how long it would take to get a couple of stitches.

Down at the farm, there's a man standing doing something, maybe coiling a rope, in the courtyard. I shout across the fence that I need a hand and he tells me to wait where I am while he gets his van. I sit down, then lie down at the side of the road. Then my knee gets sore. I sit up and prod about through the mud while the van pulls up next to me and the man gets an old sheet to cover the passenger seat. I ask the man to hide my bike behind a hedge, he sensibly ignores me and hoicks it over a wall into the farm. Actually, my leg looks pretty bad. For want of anything cleaner, I take a glove off and press it against my knee to stop the blood, then climb into the impossibly high passenger seat.

The drive takes forever. It's 15 miles to the nearest hospital. We chat about cycling and how it's getting popular in the Tweed valley, but I don't feel like talking much. I feel sick. I'm cursing my own stupidity. Why wasn't I more careful? Why didn't I slow down? Is my bike OK?

In the hospital, I'm taken into a consultation room...leaving a trail of mud behind. I'm told to lie down. 10 minutes later a doctor comes in and mumbles hello and asks what happened. After this he stares silently at my leg for a while.....thinking.

The conclusion he comes to is that I need a shower. He disappears.

Two nurses appear. They help me hobble around the corner and into a staff shower, where I get undressed and while being propped up by the giggliest nurse try to get clean. She grabs the shower head and points it into the holes in my leg. Mud and blood stream out and for the first time I see how bad it looks. With all my dignity washed down the drain. I put my t-shirt and boxers back on and make it back to the now magically cleaned up, consultation room.

A new doctor appears and gives an audible sigh before putting on a glove, grabbing a bottle of iodine, and then roughly sticking his fingers into the hole in my knee and vigorously wobbling it around while pouring the iodine in. I think I might faint.

I'm taken off to get some X-rays before coming back to the consultation room to wait. A new doctor appears and gives me the news. My knee is fine, nothing too much damaged, just some bad cuts on the front which will need an operation to clear out the mud as there's an infection risk. He tells me I need to get up, "you can stand on it, there's nothing wrong with it", and come up to a ward to wait for the op which should happen today.

I try to stand, but can't, it's too painful. The doctor disapprovingly asks a nurse to wheelchair me up to the ward.

A couple of days later after a small operation to clean up the wound, they are happy that there's no infection. I'm set up with an articulated leg brace. As long as I can accomplish the tasks a physio has set for me, then I can go. I'm wheeled down to an exercise room. As the physio watches, I hobble about, then she points at some steps, "Climb them and you're done". I wince in pain as I slowly climb each step. "Come on! There's nothing wrong with you. Get up there." I eventually make it, then turn and come back down. I'm almost crying with pain.

Two weeks later I'm at home where I grab my crutches. It's time to get my stitches out. My knee is still swollen and sore.....as far as I can tell this is normal. I get to the medical centre just around the corner from my house where the nurse looks at my knee with widening eyes before telling me I need to see a GP upstairs immediately after the stitches have been removed.

The GP tells me something isn't right and sends me to straight to A&E where I have to wait for a few hours, watching drunks pestering the staff, and idiots moaning to the receptionist about the time it's taking for someone to look at their minor ailments. In time, a young doctor shows me the X-rays from weeks previously. He asks what I can see. I point to the obvious lines showing across my knee cap and he nods and tells me I have broken my kneecap twice. He doesn't understand how it was missed. Later a more senior doctor appears and takes a look. He thinks I might not have broken my kneecap. They take a couple of new x-rays and an appointment is made for me to see a specialist the next day. On the way out the young doctor whispers conspiratorially to me "you've broken your kneecap!!"

I go to the specialist. My kneecap is in pieces.
A week later I get an MRI on my knee to check for any other damage deeper in my knee. The operator hands me a card with a list of available music on it. In amongst all the terrible choices I see only one decent option, Led Zeppelin, which obviously I choose. The operator gets me to lie down on the moving base of the MRI and straps my leg down. She hands me some 'ear-protector-ear-phones' and explains that the machine is quite noisy. Then she disappears. The machine starts up, as does the music: 'Uptown girl'.......and not even the Billy Joel version! It may have been....Westlife? It finally gets to the end of the track. I wait to hear what the next surprise will be.....it's 'Uptown girl' again! And so it continues for 45 minutes.

Finally, after seeing a specialist one more time, I'm sent on my way after being told that it's all looking surprisingly good. The bone is miraculously beginning to heal without needing to be pinned. However, the amount of time that passes while I'm not able to exercise my leg means that the muscle wastes away. My damaged leg also becomes oddly very hairy, almost werewolf like. My girlfriend finds this hilarious and tells everyone she can.

Cue a 'Rocky' style montage as I recover, switching from crutches, to one crutch, to walking, to the first painful turn of the pedals on an exercise bike, to finally getting back on a bike. Eventually, my leg returns to its pre-injury relatively thinly haired state.

As for the man at the farm who helped me out and gave me a lift. I found out the address of the farm and sent him a very nice bottle of whisky.

Hunter S. Thompson wrote: "Life should not be a journey to the grave with the intention of arriving safely in a pretty and well preserved body, but rather to skid in broadside in a cloud of smoke, thoroughly used up, totally worn out, and loudly proclaiming 'Wow! What a ride!'".

Coast to Coast route:

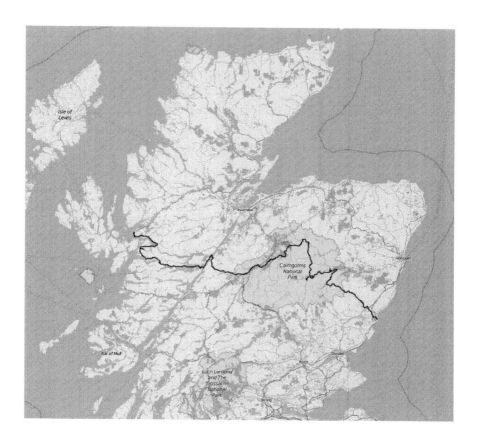

Coast-to-Coast off-road

It started at work, as most of my adventures do. For some bizarre reason, this particular day my work wasn't fully holding my attention. Maybe it was during a well-deserved tea break that the seed of a small adventure was planted. Or maybe it was the monotony of the tasks I had planned out before me that pushed me towards browsing the web for something more interesting.

Searching for new mountain bike routes, I came across a web site with a longer, more challenging route. Starting in Kyle of Lochalsh in the north-west and crossing the widest part of Scotland to reach the east coast in Montrose, it looked good. It promised adventure, beauty and excellent mountain biking, all contained within a five to seven day long, 270 kilometre mostly off-road route.

The more of the route description I read, the more interested I became. I'd never really contemplated the possibility of a multi-day mountain biking trip before, but as I read on, it seemed like a pretty good way to spend a holiday. I clicked on the 'buy' link, filled in more personal details than seemed necessary, and excitedly ordered the small accompanying guide book being offered. Afterwards, I could think of nothing else but how great cycling for a full week would be, the sun on my face, free from worries, living in the moment. I was rudely awakened from daydreaming by my desk phone ringing. I answered it, and got back to the reality of my job.

A week later, I wearily returned from work and pushed the heavy green door of my tenement flat open to find a small parcel lying on the floor within.

Opening the padded, over-taped-up package, I pulled out a small printed book with a plastic cover. Flicking though the contents revealed a book with route descriptions and a set of rough looking, hand drawn, map cards. This was going to take a bit of work to figure the route out accurately.

I scoured the required OS maps on my laptop, happily printing off the required sections before hand plotting the route from the cards and description. Checking the names of the places I'd pass through, counting contour lines to figure out the heights and steepness of various climbs. Following paths with my finger to see if there's any interesting diversions along the way. I've always like looking at maps, even places I'll never visit. Keeping an eye out for ridiculous names such as Dull (Perthshire), Hillo'manystanes (Lybster), Fattiehead (Banffshire) and Brokenwind (Aberdeenshire). Then, once I'd finished...I got distracted by the vagaries of modern life and, for a while, did nothing more.

Months later, while chatting online to an old flatmate, Sara, who had since moved back to Denmark, she mentioned that she'd bought a mountain bike. While clearly not a mountainous country (A quick web search shows the highest hill is Yding Skovhøj in central Jutland at 172m), she'd had enough fun riding track roads, and footpaths to realise that she wanted to try some more challenging rides.

We'd been cycling together before, but just on short cycles exploring around Edinburgh. We had previously shared a flat with two others; an older, disillusioned teacher called James who had three main topics of conversation; communism, bikes and his hatred of the children he had to teach. He was an interesting character though, and from him I learnt about the Glasgow uprising in 1919, called the "socialist revolution" by some. 60,000 workers committee members and trade unionists were protesting long working hours among other things. The resulting riot with the police, and failed attempts to control the protesters, culminated in the Home Secretary, Winston Churchill, who was concerned about a revolution igniting, deploying 10,000 soldiers with tanks, machine guns and howitzers! The riots were suppressed but the protesters got their reduced hours.

James also talked a lot about bikes, apparently he had an expensive full suspension bike back at his house in the countryside but I got the feeling that he rarely, if ever, actually used it.

The other flatmate owned the flat and worked in an office where apparently he literally did nothing all day. He was pretty smug about it for some reason. I'd have been bored out of my mind. I never felt comfortable hanging around his flat while he was there. So I didn't really spend any time there.

Sara rented the smallest room in the flat and had been in Edinburgh for a year's placement working at the major local newspaper. Occasionally I helped make up rushed last minute reviews of a range of things such as phones and toasters. We'd drink wine while quickly making stuff up from the features lists on the boxes. I don't remember if we actually got anything interesting enough to spend more than a few minutes testing, although we did once have a 'toaster race'. We each picked several toasters, plugged them into to various extension leads and set them all going at once. We ate a lot of toast that day...while hiding from an irate flatmate who was annoyed by the triggering of the smoke alarm, and the amount of electricity (included in our rent) we were presumably using.

We ended our online call by deciding to meet up at the end of summer. "How about a bike ride?" I asked. "I've got a guide book for a week long ride I'd like to have a go at."
I suggested the coast-to-coast. I mentioned that it'll be quite hilly. Sara replied that she was up for a bit of a challenge.

Soon, she'd booked some flights back to Scotland and I'd organised some time off of work.

Days of planning on my part then took place. Booking trains was easy, trying to find somewhere to stay for the five nights of the trip was not. The guide book recommended places, but given that I'd left this task quite late, they were often full up. It didn't help that the route was often intersected by other routes such as the busy Great Glen walk which stretches 117 kilometres across the natural fault-line dividing the northern highlands from the Grampian highlands. The popularity of the route being due to the landscapes created by the interactions between two tectonic plates along the fault. The rocks to the north were previously part of the same tectonic plate on which the Appalachian mountains in the northern US are formed. The fault line is also responsible for creating the second deepest, and monster-iest water in Britain, Loch Ness.

The lodgings mentioned in the guide that weren't booked up generally either no longer existed or were closed. Anyway, with a bit of persistence and some route changes, a variety of accommodation was booked.

Finally the first day of the trip was nearly upon us. After finishing work and making my way home, I stayed up late packing, then unpacking, discarding several of the less important items before packing again.

    The following morning I was woken ridiculously early by my girlfriend grumpily shaking me awake after I'd ignored the first time my alarm went off and hit 'sleep' for another ten minutes of comfort. I got up, skipping breakfast as it was too early to feel hungry, said goodbye, and made my way the short distance through the quiet streets to the main Edinburgh train station. Soon, I was asleep in an uncomfortable but warm seat for the three hour journey northwards.

    I arrived at Aberdeen station still far too early on a freezing cold morning. I sat next to my bike and a pile of my stuff which should have been smaller and shivered. Already the short Scottish summer was over and the weather was getting colder. I watched a rat attacking a polystyrene box of takeaway thrown away into a dark corner. A few people strode purposefully along the platforms. No-body else was hanging around in the cold for long.

    Eventually Sara arrived from the airport already looking exhausted from the struggle of flying with a bike and getting it from the airport into the centre of town.

"Sara!! You made it!" I said, arms outstretched.

"Of course. The taxi wouldn't let me take my bike though. Some guy gave me a lift", she said in that familiar Danish accent that sounds a bit like someone going down a slide; high to low. The café at the back of the station was open. We went for some coffee to warm up and waited the hour until the next train arrived.

    Comparing our loads, we realised that we could have easily

saved on at least some of the weight, we now had double sets of heavy tools and spare tubes, and probably other things as well. Well, we were both here, which was miraculous given our general lack of organisation, so it was a pretty good start.

Soon enough it was time to catch the next train through the farmlands of the north-east, the area in which I grew up, before continuing west into the highlands.

At Inverness we had to change again, this time there was a worryingly large group of cyclists trying to get on the same train as us. Scotrail generally have room for about 4-6 bikes on each train, all jammed together and strapped to the wall in a cramped space next to the toilets. It surprisingly works quite well. Having panniers makes the parking manoeuvre much trickier. An act impossible to pull off without annoying other passengers as bike luggage is temporarily dumped into the walkway while the bikes are dealt with. The worst part though is if you are getting off and someone else has put their bike on top. This results in a sort of less than beautiful bike ballet accompanied by a soundtrack of swearwords and pain.

Finally the train arrived and, as expected, the group of cyclists piled on. Luckily, for once in my life I'd been organised and not only had I booked tickets for ourselves, but I'd booked the bikes onto each of the trains for our whole outwards trip. The conductor gave us priority and told some of the group there was no room.

We quickly made sure our bikes were on, then noticing the conductor had wandered off, we helped some of the others pile their bikes on top. There were a few tense moments until the train departed in case the conductor returned. But when he did it was too late to throw anyone off, we were well on our way.

This section of railway was completed in 1897 after a struggle with nature which made this, at the time, the most expensive section of railway to be built in the UK. Twenty-nine new bridges had to be constructed and thirty-one excavations through solid rock had to be dug in a relatively short distance. It was primarily built to speed the transport of livestock and fish from the west coast to markets which otherwise previously took several days by boat. Now it carries tourists.

We settled in and I pulled the maps out and spread them across the table. There was enough room to align them between cardboard cups of tea to show each day's planned route. It was the first time Sara had seen our itinerary for the week. I showed her the first day and where we'd be stopping. It didn't look like too hard a start to our ride.

The views out of the train windows as we passed through remote sections on the journey west, were stunning. The purple heather was at its end of summer brightest. The sun was shining on the lochs and pine forests. We spotted a herd of deer, staying close to the safety of the trees. The train plodded along through the hills with no sense of urgency. There were few stops. When we did, we found ourselves looking out at tiny, pretty, stations with nothing more than a few buildings scattered around. Almost three hours later we were close to our destination, passing the picturesque settlement of Plockton on the rocky coast before bending south to the larger town of Kyle.

Kyle, or Kyle of Lochalsh to give it its full name, is the largest town in the area. As well as being the gateway to Skye, with the bridge being a mile away, it's the train terminus and home to a sizeable marina. It's also home to the British underwater Test and Evaluation Centre, or BUTEC as it's more commonly referred to. This is the facility that tests out underwater and surface based weapons and equipment for the UK military. As well as testing minesweepers and torpedoes, they controversially test low frequency sonar systems here, widely blamed for the death of whales and dolphins on mass. However, it's also thought to actually benefit the local environment in a way. The restricted test areas are a safe haven for fish to breed in, and as a result stocks are also healthy in other adjacent areas.

We pulled into the station which sticks rather strangely out into the water on a man-made quay. After disembarking and attaching our luggage onto our bikes, we pushed them up a ramp and onto the main road.

13

I was keen to do our first bit of cycling of the adventure, but I was also hungry. We scooted around the town looking for something suitable, before finally settling on getting some fish and chips from 'Hector's Plaice'. We enjoyed them while sitting overlooking the waters of the Kyle Akin sound between the mainland and Skye. A few tiny boats were making their way under the Skye bridge and heading into the safety of Loch Alsh to the east. It was a calm evening, although I noticed how quickly it was getting cold now that the sun was getting low.

Finally, full of food, we set off for our first bit of cycling. We found our way out of town and headed north. A short five kilometre stretch back in the wrong direction to a bed and breakfast. Of course it was up a massive hill. It was good though to finally turn the pedals and stretch our legs.

Following the only road north, the houses were few and spread out. The Tigh-a-Cladach announced itself with a large green sign. Welcomed in by the owner of the Bed and Breakfast I asked about where it was best to put the bikes. We were directed around the side of the building to a sheltered area. We didn't bother to lock them up as we were in the middle of nowhere. It seemed more than unlikely that someone would steal them in the night.

After fighting the luggage off of the panniers, we were shown to our rooms, sorted our stuff out (in my case I dumped my bags onto the floor and put on a warm jumper), and then went to the living room where the other guests were hanging out.

We were immediately asked all about our trip. After sheepishly telling the short tale of our five kilometre cycle so far and making it clear that we hadn't actually been anywhere yet, this being the start point, we returned the enquiry and found out all about the other's trips. Mostly they were older couples who were driving their way around the coast. A younger couple were hitching, by the sounds of it, they'd not had much trouble finding lifts so far. The chat continued for a while before the B&B owner announced he'd like to show us something and dived out the door. He soon excitedly burst back in and we were 'treated' to some accordion playing. Well at least he seemed to enjoy it. As soon as I thought I could get away with it without appearing rude, I made my excuses and went to bed early.

Day 1: Kyle - Corran

I woke up, sleepily looked at my watch and pulled back the curtains to realise that the view from my window was spectacular. The window overlooked a well-kept garden full of rocks and assorted heathers. Stretching out from the bottom of the garden was the sea and the mountains of Skye across the water. I left my room and went down the hall to the shared living space. The full breakfast I'd ordered the night before appeared. I knew it was going to be a good day.

Finally, it was time to make a start. We said goodbye to our hosts and set off along the road to Kyle. As we enjoyed the payback of rolling back down the big hill we had climbed the previous day, the views to our right were of flat, dark seas, the low sun in the east not yet penetrating the depths.

Once we had again passed through Kyle of Lochalsh, we hit possibly the busiest road of the whole journey. A lorry filled, but smooth, ride down to Sheil Bridge. Having extra weight on our bike may have actually helped to stop us falling off as the wind from the high speed traffic did it's best to knock us off. Some of the passes were ridiculously close. It's not hard to comprehend the apparent lack of common sense involved in driving like that. Cars are built to isolate you from the outside world. Comfy seats, bump absorbing suspension, warmth, radios, no fear of being hurt. Less and less effort is being required of drivers. It's easy to lose yourself and forget that anything exists outside your box and it's imaginary, seemingly unstoppable, path forwards through the landscape. Of course when you are stopped by roadworks or other traffic you crash out of this lovely world and into a world where you suddenly realise that the car is not a rush but a short-term prison.

Drivers, myself included, would possibly be more respectful of other road users if driving was a struggle. Wind rushing through the interior, suspension where you felt every bump in the road, the fear of injury if you aren't careful. Better still, we could just wait until the human driver is taken out of the loop completely and we can all enjoy reading, napping or skronking (add you own rude word here) while our self-driving car takes control.

Half way along this section of road, and sticking out into the water is the iconic Eilean Donan castle, as seen in many a film, and a staple calendar image and probably one of the most photographed buildings in Scotland.

We stopped in the car park for a break from the traffic and found a grassy spot to dump the bikes and have a sit down. Sara had a grumble about the traffic. In Denmark bikes are sensibly kept apart from the cars as much as possible. There are at least 7000 kilometres of proper bike lanes. Even most country roads, and certainly all newish roads, have cycle lanes. Often these are physically separated (rather than just a painted line) and raised higher than the rest of the road. Riding on a busy road, like we currently were doing, must seem insane to Danes.

We took a look around the outside of the castle which sticks out into Loch Alsh. The castle as seen isn't actually that old. The original was demolished in 1719 by the Royal Navy as it was a stronghold for the failed Jacobite uprising and their Spanish support. After some intense gun-fighting, the Navy finally captured the castle. It then took two days and many barrels of gunpowder to destroy it. A photo of the castle from around 1909 shows not much of it is left. It was restored in 1932, when a bridge was also built to the small island it sits on.

We braved the road once again. By now it was at least a little quieter. Maybe the morning rush was over? Even so, we were thankful to reach the turn off ten kilometres further on at Sheil Bridge. Here we pedalled onto a small, quiet road which lead back along the opposite side of the sea Loch towards Glen Elg. In front of us was Sgurr Mhic Bharraich, a steep sided mountain. Although reaching a height of only 779 metres, its sudden emergence from the

17

wide, flat, sea level estuary we were crossing made it appear more impressive than otherwise. We cycled across flat farmland, nosily rattled over a couple a cattle grids, and headed ominously towards the mountain. On reaching the base, the road suddenly headed upwards at a frankly absurd angle. The difference in effort required to keep moving was quite a shock. I hadn't expected to need to use my lowest gear quite so soon. I stopped on the very first corner, it was as if my body just refused to comprehend the work now required of it. Even just standing still took some effort, the hill was so steep the weight of my stationary bike was pulling me backwards. I took my jacket off and stuffed it into the top of a pannier. Sara pulled up next to me with a 'bloody hell!'. I took a drink of water, took a deep breath and with a wobble set off again. The steepest section came a bit later as we twisted up around some sharp bends. This would be a tough enough climb without a heavy load of equipment in panniers.

Regretting the weight of the multiple pairs of underpants in my bags, I pushed onwards, slowly grinding the pedals around and breathing heavily. Sara dropped back a bit but wasn't giving in either. The view on the road was great though and became even better towards the top as it opened out to display the whole loch below, mountains to the north, and Kyle of Lochalsh below. Although we'd been cycling for a few hours, the double back around the sea loch meant we were quite close to where we started. As the road finally flattened out, we stopped again to catch our breath.

"Well, this is unexpectedly hard" pointed out Sara.

"Yeah, today was supposed to be a gentle start...and this is when we are climbing on nice smooth tarmac, we're not even off-road yet!"

Despite the tough climb, I was loving this as much as I'd hoped.

After the final gentle climb and a bit of flat road through a forest came the inevitable downhill, and this one was awesome. Dropping quickly between two steep sided hills, the muted browns of the heather bordering the road soon turned to luscious, grassy greens. The road worked its way down the side of a beautiful, wide glacial valley. A metal crash barrier was all that separated us from a steep drop off to the left.

The hills to the far side of the valley looked untouched by man. No roads, fields or masts to be seen. Just large swathes of thick forest of uniform green except for shadowy indents from which the brightest light from the sun was banished. In the past, these remote areas would have been far from empty. On cold days the smoke from multiple crofts would have been seen as fires burned warming farming families.

It was in these hills where the story of an unhappy farmer called John McInnes was set. He struggled with the day-to-day labours of his farm until, one day, a mysterious figure appeared and said he'd send a fine horse to help John out, as long as he stuck to certain rules. Soon after, a farie water-horse (or 'Each-Uisge' in galic) appeared and John set it to ploughing and other tasks around the farm. One version of the story says that John spread earth from a molehill on the horse's back every night as a charm to stop it escaping. Maybe this was one of the rules set by the mysterious figure...who knows? Anyway, the farmer apparently forgot to do this one night. The horse noticed, grabbed him in its teeth and ran into a small loch, neither of them was seen again! And the moral is....don't forget to spread moley earth over your magical horse or it'll get you.

With the terrible smell of burning brakes, we soon arrived at the valley floor and continued on for a few miles to the tiny hamlet of Glen Elg. There were a few spread out buildings and a hotel, appropriately called the Glen Elg Inn. Further investigation proved fruitful in that we found it had a nice bar. After locking up the bikes and buying some drinks, we sat out in the garden overlooking the loch and enjoying the sun. It was surprisingly busy with people enjoying lunch, and loads of kids running about. The weather was perfect for sitting drinking beer and looking out to sea. Reading the guide book and checking our route on the maps we decided to wait till later for food as there was a café listed next to where we were booked to stay the night. We weren't exactly in any hurry to move

19

on though and decided to stay put for a while and enjoy another pint in the sun.

Finally, we worked up enough energy to make a move and continued down the road where, after a short distance, we made a detour to visit a couple of brochs. I dumped my heavy panniers in the undergrowth at the end of the small road so I didn't have to carry them up the steep hill. The difference was amazing. I zoomed ahead up the hill feeling like Lance Armstrong at the height of his cheating.

We came to the first of the amazing broch structures. These are defensive, windowless, tower-like roundhouses built from drystone usually around 100BC-100AD. In fact they are some of the most complex structures constructed without any 'glue' such as cement or lime and are unique to Scotland. At over twenty metres in diameter, with passages and stairs within, considerable effort must have been put into their construction. They are thought to have had various uses such as storing grains as well as having living space for a family or community. I'd never seen these close up before so took a good look around and climbed some of the internal stairs up to the top of the ten metre high wall remnants. The single entrance hole in the outer wall was usually secured with a thick wooden door barricaded by heavy wooden beams which slotted into the wall behind, enough to stop most attackers. It must have been pretty good to be inside these safe walls on a stormy night, or when rival groups were trying to pillage.

We cycled a bit further up the hill to see the other broch and sat for a while on a wall by the ruin eating some cereal bars and taking in the view.

There are many remaining mysteries concerning brochs. The age of the structures means that we'll never know for sure for what purpose they were built, and how the same basic design came to be used at disparate locations throughout Scotland and the islands.

Re-energised, we pushed on along the coast road past Sandaig. This is the near mythical place where Gavin Maxwell lived and wrote his autobiographical account of his life living with otters "Ring of bright water", first published in 1960. He's buried here along with 'Edal', his otter who died in a fire which also destroyed the cottage. Edal was the otter responsible for biting several fingers off of the naturalist and TV presenter Terry Nutkins. He presented 'The Really Wild Show' when I was a kid. When he was younger, he lived with Maxwell for several years to help look after the otters. Apparently, one day a woman who was disliked by the otters, gave a jumper to the young Nutkins, who was then attacked when they smelt the jumper.

We didn't visit the house remains as they are a bit of a walk from the road, but if we had then we would have easily spotted the curved river from which the books title is derived. We'd also have seen the waterfall to which Gavin said he would return after death.

We rode past and continued down one of the most beautiful parts of coastline I've seen. The sun was shining and the deep, Mediterranean, blue of the sea contrasted with the purple of the heather growing on the rocky islands. I stopped to take a photo. It made a great picture. I've still got it, hanging in my hallway. We rolled down a hill past an old church and took our time gently pedalling along the untaxing road towards one of the remotest villages in Scotland, Corran.

Several miles further, we passed a small group of highland cows grazing at the edges of the road. Despite their size, wild look, hairy, eye-less faces and long horns ending in sharp points, these animals, possibly because of their confidence in the fact that nothing would dare mess with them, are usually benign. We passed between them. They didn't even look up from their meal.

We made it Corran earlier than expected and decided to visit the café.

The 'café' turned out to be a shed in the garden of the B&B we'd booked into. It was closed. We went around to the house where, after knocking on the door, a lady answered and introduced herself as Sheila. It quickly became apparent that she was the owner of the B&B and wasn't expecting us even though it must have been her I'd spoken to on the phone a few days before. She was also disconcerted about having a male and a female staying in her house. After explaining that we weren't sharing a room like she'd at first thought, she seemed to relax.

I asked about food and she said she didn't have any, we'd have to wait until breakfast. I pointed out that her sign said the café should be open, and after the longest sigh I've ever heard she said she could make us some sandwiches, but made it abundantly clear that the effort would probably kill her.

That evening the weather was beautiful. I didn't fancy spending it in the dingy, dark living room watching the tiny tv. Sara was reading a book and didn't fancy going for a walk, so it was just me and the midges.

A few people were out, all of them had midge hoods on. One of them had a full body midge suit which I've never seen before. But my god they were needed. The midges were insane. I've only seen them this bad in one other place, a boggy camp-site on Skye. Forced to run, I quickly reached the pebble beach which was slightly less migified. Walking along the coast a slight breeze cleared the worst of the bitey little beasties.

I rounded a corner on the beach to find it covered in odd little stone constructions. People had created towers of stones by balancing them on top of each other, the stones getting smaller on the way up. Somehow, unless someone had been very busy that morning, these fragile looking things appeared to be able to withstand the weather. I had to build one.

It took me about an hour of stone searching, several failed attempts, and precise positioning to get a tower built. Minuscule differences in how the rocks were positioned would make the difference between a sculpture and a shambolic pile of stones. Feeling like I'd achieved something, I headed back to the B&B.

Day 2: Corran – Fort Augustus

With legs feeling a bit achy I awoke to the smell of breakfast and the
B&B owner shuffling about in the living room. Much as I'd have
liked to lounge around in bed for a bit, the aroma was too powerful
and I quickly got up and dressed before heading through. Given the
quality of the sandwiches the night before I wasn't expecting much.
But this lady knew how to cook a breakfast, and made masses of
bacon, eggs and beans for us. Even proper coffee. With all this food
it was becoming clear why she might think no-one needs to eat for
the rest of the day.

Stepping outside of the B&B the air was freezing, but it was
otherwise a beautiful, bright morning. The midges had disappeared.
We took our time reloading the bikes before taking some photos of
the village and surrounding scenery. Then we took some more
photos of our bikes in front of the scenery. Finally, we said goodbye
to Sheila and set off. After a very short distance, we turned a corner
only to be stopped by a massive stag blocking our way. It was
standing in the middle of the street looking into space. However, it
didn't seem at all bothered so we gingerly made our way around
him and his huge antlers before continuing on our way. I wonder
what he was thinking about?

The route started with our first proper bit of off-roading up Glen
Arnisdale. We left the well-worn road and headed up the valley on
some very rough track. As we climbed higher and the trees
thickened from a heathery stubble to a full beard of a forest, the
sheltered and windless track allowed the midges to cloud. They
were again driving us insane but at least it didn't last long. Soon the
trees thinned out and our benevolent saviour, the breeze, returned.
The track road soon turned to single track path covered in mud. It

was mostly cyclable, but every so often we'd have to dismount and negotiate our way around some obstacle, usually sections of deep mud.

It was good to be out in the wilderness miles from anyone. I was really enjoying this trip, it just kept getting better. This is what I love to do. Nothing beats being outdoors with nothing to worry about apart from what to eat for lunch and reaching that night's bed. Sara was also clearly enjoying this more than the tarmac road and we chatted about nonsense as we made our way between the hills and around lochs. Even as the path became soft and un-cycleable our spirits were high. We were now following an old drove road. In the past, cattle from the island of Skye were boated across to Glenelg (where we'd stopped at the pub the day before), before they were driven south along this route to be sold at market.

A short push later and the path improved and headed downwards once again. It soon turned into a track road with an awesome steep twisty downhill which again tested our brakes. This was the best of mountain biking. We skidded and slid downwards for a short, but fun, few minutes. Before us we could see the valley opening out and stretching out eastwards, although I was too busy concentrating on the track in front of me to enjoy the view.

We reached the farm at Kinloch Hourn (or 'Ceann Loch Shubhairne' in Galic, which literally means 'the head of Loch Hourne') and a small track road. This is the very end of the road, a few cars were parked nearby. Presumably they were owned by walkers exploring the remote paths which continue to the west and into the great road-less vastness of the Knoydart peninsula. We continued on along the quiet road, surrounded by heather and old trees, for miles and miles of lovely cycling.

Eventually we reached Loch Quoich and followed the edge of the water before reaching the imposing Glen Quoich dam. There was an existing loch before the dam, but the huge structure raised the water by 30 metres and increased the surface area from three to seven square miles. It was built to provide hydro power in 1955 and at the time was by far the biggest dam of its type; rock-filled, reinforced with concrete and then faced with natural stone. A huge engineering feat.

A little further down the road we reached the Tomdoun hotel where we stopped for a rest and to see if we could get some food. We were too late for the official lunch menu, but they kindly made us some amazing sandwiches to go with our beer. We ate while listening in to a conversation the barman was having with a customer about ticks, how he'd had one the day before right in his belly button, and how there seemed to be many more this year than normal. I started scratching at the thought and resolved to check my bare legs more often.

My daughter once, after a walk in the countryside, complained of a "tummy bug". We asked if she felt sick or wanted to go to bed but instead she lifted her top and pointed to an actual bug. A tick!

On another cycling trip, a friend and I came to visit the loch a short distance north of the hotel, Loch Loyne. Every September the water is drained in preparation for the winter rain and snow. This exposes the old 'Road to the Isles' which used to be the main road to Kyle of Lochalsh before it, and its humpbacked bridges, were submerged by the building of a dam. Anyway, we'd come in the hope of being able to experience the interesting phenomenon of cycling across the apparently well preserved route. Five hours of driving, a night of camping in a quiet lay-by, and a couple of hours of cycling later we finally arrived at the loch to find it..........completely full of water! The road disappeared at our side and then tantalisingly reappeared off in the distance. Maybe I'll come back and try again another year. We ended up doing an alternative route that was amazing anyway.

After finally leaving the comfort of the hotel, we re-mounted and quickly covered the short distance downhill to the end of the road at Invergarry. Here we joined the Great glen way. A popular off-road coast-to-coast walking and cycling route. The 73 mile long route follows the course of the Caledonian Canal and it's interlinking lochs as it makes it way from Fort William in the west to Inverness in the east. We followed the undulating and rough path for five kilometres until we reached Bridge of Oich where the guide book told us to take the canal path.

By now it was getting late. We'd been taking our time all afternoon and somehow hadn't covered much distance since our late lunch. Now, presented with a completely flat, smooth surface to ride on, we floored it. The canal path seemed long and a bit of a chore compared to the riding before, and we were glad to finally reach Fort Augustus and the Youth Hostel.

After dumping our smelly stuff in the common dormitory, I had a shower. I say shower, but it was a miserable cold dribble. I'd have been better off jumping in a loch earlier on.

Not really refreshed or clean, it was time to go find some food. We found a nearby pub which looked decent and I filled up on a steak and ale pie with chips. A pint finished things off and after a relaxing few hours off of the bikes we headed off to bed.

Day 3: Fort Augustus - Newtonmore

After a not bad night's sleep considering the sleeping arrangements, I got up. For some reason I felt terrible. I'd not had too much to drink, and yesterday, while long, hadn't been too taxing. Maybe I was coming down with something. My body was trying to tell me to stay in bed. Instead, I got up and packed my stuff ready for a tough day.

Today we were going over the famous Corrieyairack pass, topping out at 770m. The route over the pass follows General Wade's military road. It was built in 1731 in order to allow troops to move quickly. While Commander in Chief of the army of northern Britain, Wade visited the highlands and found them to be in "a state of anarchy and confusion". Impossible to access and control with his troops, he decided to build both new Garrisons to house troops, and roads between, to allow ease of movement across, and through, the mountains and moors. The pass includes the highest point of the General's road.

Ironically the first people to use the road in a time of war, were not the army who built it, but the opposing Jacobites.

We ate a leisurely breakfast of rolls and marmalade along with several mugs of tea. After a trip to a small shop to resupply, we finally headed off through the early morning fog, along a quiet back road.

Ten minutes after starting out we were confused. We were supposed to turn off onto a track road which ran through a forest. However, where there there was only one track marked on the map, in reality there were several, heading off in slightly different directions. Which one was the real one?

I wanted to just go for the track which looked the best used.

"Looking at the map, that one to the left seems like it's going in the right direction" said Sara.

"Umm...ok, let's just flip a coin" I suggested.

Sara agreed. I dug out a coin from my pocket and flipped it. "Let's go!" Sara said, jumping back on her bike and pedalling away. I set off following Sara as she disappeared off around a corner. Turns out it was the correct road.

The road soon got steep. I rode past Sara as she stopped for a breather. A bit further on, after emerging form the pine forest, I spotted a group of mountain bikers slowly working their way up a long steep section ahead. I was enjoying the remoteness of the track and so, not fancying cycling along in a big group, I stopped to wait and to give them a chance to get further ahead. It wasn't long before Sara arrived. She was now powering along the track. Together we struggled upwards. Soon enough, we were passing the tail-enders of the cycle group, breathlessly saying 'hello' as we passed. They weren't carrying anything apart from some tiny rucksacks and had some quite nice, expensive looking, bikes. The aching in my legs gradually increased as I worked my way up, wobbling as I navigated my front wheel between the sizeable rocks strewn across the track. Balancing at this slow speed with panniers on the back was also proving a challenge. Further up the hill, gravity finally beat us. I had to get off and push up the steepest, roughest, section.

I caught up with one of the group who'd also given up on cycling and was now stopped, facing back down the hill, taking in the view while leaning in his bike. "Wow....you've made it up here with all that stuff on yer bikes?" he said in a Canadian accent. He appeared to be genuinely impressed. Further conversation revealed his name was James and that he was doing the same route as us as part of a week-long guided package. "So how are you enjoying it so far?" I asked. "Beautiful, beautiful!" he replied. I wasn't sure if he was referring to the cycling or the scenery.

"You can't have many spare clothes for the day, you don't seem to be carrying anything?"

"Nah, it's ok, the minibus is just at the other side."

It turns out they were only riding the best sections of the route while missing out the more sedate or tedious sections. They were taking the minibus the rest of the way. Sounded like a fun way of doing it to me. Saving more energy for the more interesting and exciting sections.

We decided to have lunch at the top along with the rest of the group and spent a while chatting in the sun, looking forwards to the downhill before us.

Before General Wade's arrival, the route through the pass had been a drover's road. The grassy flat summit we were now sitting on was used to rest and give the cattle a chance to graze. After the building of the road, the new surface was at first welcomed by the drovers, but soon they changed their minds as they discovered the road surface was damaging the hooves of the cattle.

Off we set once more. This time no pedalling was required. For a few glorious minutes it was fun. Then the road surface turned from what had been relatively smooth track road, to a rocky nightmare. The road surface had been destroyed by many years of being washed out by snow melt and rain water. The boulders are all that's left of the original surface of General Wade's road. All the smaller stuff that had been packed between the giant stones to create a smoother surface has long ago disappeared. Rarely is going downhill so frustrating. The group of bikers quickly left us behind, their lack of weight and better bikes with decent suspension allowing the wheels to silently bounce over the rocks while keeping the rider steady on top.

We struggled on down the track, sometimes bumping, sometimes pushing, sometimes lifting. We reached the well know zig-zags down the steepest section of hillside. The road surface improved here and became more hard packed and grassy. As we raced down this fun section rolling fast, then braking hard at each corner, I counted. I'd reached twelve by the time the track straightened out.

The road continued in a dead straight line, ignoring any contours in the hillside as it descended. The surface was once again horrible to ride on. So we had to frustratingly push for large sections as we made our way down.

After a long time, we reached the much improved track at the bottom of the hill. Now we could roll, and it was brilliant. We flew down the remainder of the rough road before reaching the single-track tarmac at Garva Bridge where it was easy riding. We had taken much longer than expected to get across the Corrieyairack pass so when we reached the small village of Laggan at the end of the road, we decided to take a small detour to a hotel for some food and a rest. It was a bit grim. The bar was empty but for one dishevelled fellow leaning on the tiny bar. I ordered a sandwich and coke and we sat in the bright, soul-less room wondering how places like this survive. The outside of the building had shown so much promise, being a grand looking Victorian building with the ruins of an old church in the large garden. I guess being the only hotel/bar in the area had allowed the owner to become lax in the upkeep of the place.

Looking at the guide book. We didn't have far to go. Finally I plundered my last remaining energy reserves and we headed off for the last ten kilometres along the main road to the small town of Newtonmore, where we were to stay the night.

Thanks to the small size of the town and the large size of the sign, we easily found the hostel on the main street. Wheeling the bikes up the short driveway, the owner appeared. He cheerily asked us where we'd come from and so we regaled him with the short story of our day on the pass.

He told us that he competed in a race over the pass every year, the 'Corrieyairack challenge', apparently one of the country's toughest, but short-ish, duathalons. It crosses the pass with a choice of running of mountain biking (not as unfair as it sounds, I think running would be probably be faster) and then returns by bike back to the start along 39 miles of roads. "Come with me, you might be interested in this!" he said beckoning us around the side of the building. He took us to his double garage, opening the door to

reveal lots and lots of bikes neatly hanging up on racks at the back, all of which were his. He grinned while watching for our reaction, "What do you think?" A few of the bikes were clearly junk, but the majority seemed like decent or at least interesting old bikes.
"I try to ride them each at least once every year" he said.
"Which one is your favourite?" I asked.
He pointed to a modern red road bike that couldn't have been more than a couple of years old. Fair enough.

That night we stayed in the entirely empty hostel. We had a large choice of rooms so spent a few minutes exploring before choosing the most comfortable ones. We didn't have any food so a quick trip to the small co-op just down the road was in order. The hostel had a good kitchen with everything we could possibly need, so there weren't any restrictions on what we could cook. Sara fancied having some chips and a pie, I wanted some pasta in the hope that it would re-energise me for the next day. We compromised, and got both. As well as a couple of bottles of beer each.

It was nice to have a quiet night in. We sat in the comfy shared living area drinking beer, chatting and reading, before heading off to bed, exhausted and slightly woozy.

Day 4: Newtonmore – Tomintoul

After an excellent night's sleep in the quiet of the empty hostel and a long lie in, followed by lots of toast and coffee, we set off along the cycle path from Newtonmore to Kingussie, five kilometres away.

I knew this was going to be quite a long day as we had to get to Tomintoul and, after examining the map, it looked like a lot of the route was off-road. This first section was easy enough though. We turned onto a small back road at Kingussie, and waited for about ten minutes in the cold at a train crossing, before the two-carriage long train actually came through at crawling speed. Finally the barriers lifted and we warmed up as we got pedalling. It wasn't long before we stopped once more. This time, for a quick visit to the impressive and ruined Ruthven Barracks. This was an accommodation building for 120 troops led by the Duke of Cumberland, strategically positioned to stop any future Jacobite uprisings as well as attempting, and pretty much failing, to maintain law and order between the feisty local clans. It was built on top of a probably far more interesting fortified castle from 1229. The most interesting story is from 1745 when several hundred Jacobites attacked the barracks which happened at that moment to only have twelve people inside. Presumably the twelve were panic-stricken, but they somehow successfully defended the building while losing only a single soldier.   It certainly left them with a good story to tell the returning soldiers, "you'll never believe what happened while you were out!"

We continued along the quiet back road as it undulated its way along the side of the river Spey. The flat, marshy valley bottom to our left dramatically and slowly expanded out until it formed Loch Insh, with its water sports centre. A visit to which, appears to be mandatory for almost every child in Scotland. I was almost drowned there when I fell out of a boat wearing the wellies my parents had made me wear. "No you can't wear trainers, boots will keep your feet dry!" Inevitably, they filled with water and dragged me down until I kicked them off. Of course, I then got in trouble for losing them after a nearby canoeist returned me, bedraggled, to the shore.

It wasn't long before it was time to turn off of the tarmac and back onto forest track at Feshiebridge. The road was difficult to navigate, turnings going off in all directions. It was slow progress stopping and checking the route at each junction.

Eventually, we successfully escaped the maze and reached Loch an Eilein where the track turned to a thin path along the beautiful waterside. It was voted Britain's best picnic spot in 2010, by whom, I don't know. I'd have liked to be one of the judges though. We were now at the edge of the well-known Rothiemurchus estate.

Rothiemurchus is a managed estate, full of Scots pine and well maintained paths. It's supposedly one of the largest areas of ancient woodland in Europe with the average age of the trees well over 100 years. The oldest trees are over 300 years old. It seems to be better managed than many estates, the usual policies of killing every animal apart from grouse not being enacted, meaning it's home to a diverse range of wildlife such as capercaillies, osprey, red squirrels, woodpeckers and even the occasional wildcat. It's certainly a beautiful place to pass through.

We were cutting right across the middle of the estate. We stopped to take some photos of us looking rugged and adventurous riding through the rivers trying not to fall in, posing next to squiggly tree trunks and stuffing sandwiches into our faces. The Estate is relatively flat as well which made a nice change from the previous few days. It was busy with walkers, a few of which stopped to chat.

We cycled on around the very edge of the Cairngorms mountains and along the back of Loch Morlich before passing a camp-site and reaching the road which takes visitors up the mountain to the ski centre. Stopping for a look at the long sandy beach at the loch's edge I noticed the sand is mixed with lots of broken, but worn down and so no longer sharp, glass. I've since learnt that during the Second World War, the beach was used as a training area for the Norwegian commandos called the Kompani Linge. The glass coming from the many Molotov cocktails they threw around during training. This group became famous for their raid on the German controlled fertiliser plant at Vemork in 1943. Worried that the Germans could start up the plant and use its by-product of heavy water to develop nuclear weapons, the Norwegian commandos set out to destroy the plant. At first the plan didn't go well. Some were killed when one of the planes crashed. The others arrived silently by glider, well off target, and had to ski a long distance back to the plant, before waiting for backup while surviving on a diet of moss and lichen. Eventually, more Norwegian commandos arrived by parachute and joined up with the original group after several days of searching.

The single bridge across a deep ravine was the only easy way into the plant but was heavily guarded. The Norwegians instead descended the ravine, crossed the river at the bottom and climbed up the other side where they were able to follow a train track straight into the heart of the buildings. A friendly Norwegian janitor they came across showed them where to put the explosives, but then refused to let them light the fuses until he had found his glasses, which were irreplaceable during the war! The raid was ultimately considered successful, stopping production for a period. The commandos escaped. About half stayed nearby to help on future missions and the others skied the 400km to Sweden. Further air bombing raids were carried out to stop production permanently.

From the beach it was a short distance through some trees to the main road. We stopped for coffee at the nearby visitor centre. In the shop full of furry deer toys and skiing themed pencils, I bought a red translucent plastic mug with a picture of a pine martin as a present for my girlfriend. We still have the mug. It's a seemingly indestructible favourite. It has come on many camping trips with us.

After the stop, although happy, I was already feeling tired today. Opening the map on the table in front on me and seeing that the next bit was going to be uphill did nothing for our motivation to leave the café. However, sitting around wasn't getting us nearer to Tomintoul where we were staying the night.

Turns out leaving the café and starting cycling wasn't much better at getting us there. We took the wrong track. It was in roughly the right direction. However, it soon became apparent that we were climbing much higher than we need to be and a break in the trees revealed the correct path way down below. What would have been sensible to do at this point would have been to retrace our steps and find the right track. Instead, we did what everyone else would have done in the same situation....try to take the shorter distance down the side of a steep wooded hillside and across a bog, fighting midges all the way and swearing a lot. It wouldn't have been so bad if we were just out walking, but carrying our bikes most of the way as well as our over-abundance of stuff almost killed us.

Once back on the main track, we were soon rewarded with a beautiful small loch (An Lochan Uaine) of an eerie green colour with a wall of scree heading upwards on the opposite side.

Legend has it that the loch is green because the faeries wash their clothes in it. These creatures are naughty and mischievous pests, not the cute little fairies most would imagine. Supposedly, they live up on the mountain and if you look very carefully you can come across the little doorways from which they emerge to wreak havoc on any passers-by.

Soon after, we passed Ryvoan bothy. I'd previously stayed here with a couple of friends after walking in from Nethy Bridge. We poked our heads in the door. I was glad to see it still in use and in a good state. It was smaller than I remembered though.

On we continued through the Abernethy Forest national nature reserve crossing more shallow rivers as we went. If anything, this was even nicer to cycle through than the Rothimurchus estate. The views to our right of the mountains were spectacular and there was absolutely no-one else to be seen. For an hour or so the cycling was amazing, but it was too good to last. Our route soon turned to a small path through the heather. Then the path ended in a muddy bog with no obvious onwards route. This obviously made it difficult to navigate. The route description told us we had to head for the Braes of Abernethy, through a steep sided gully between 2 scree covered hills. Seeing what we assumed were the hills in front of us, we scrambled along what looked like a fire break in the forest. The route was in a word, terrible. Dragging our belongings over fallen trees, falling into boggy holes and otherwise struggling onwards while not being quite sure we were going the right way was not doing much for our happiness levels. A section of deep, peaty mud did its best impression of sinking sand. I pulled a leg out leaving my shoe behind, overbalanced and fell sideways, thankfully I managed to land on some big grassy tufts. After retrieving the shoe, I stopped to wash the worst of the mud off in a stream. Eventually, we popped out the other side of the woods, and miraculously, there before us was the steep pass!

The torment wasn't quite over. The path up between the hills was steep and bouldery. Impossible to cycle. Still, it was a definite improvement on what had come before. Eventually, at the top, when we could see we'd done the worst of it, we stopped for some food and to laugh about the state of our legs. Scratched to bits and covered in mud. Still, this wasn't supposed to be a 'ride in the park'.

From here we could see it was relatively flat across some moorland and fields. We blasted down the single-track. It was brilliant. It was easy.

After following some 'barely-there' tracks across some fields we came across a familiar face standing next to a mini-bus. It was one of the guys I'd spoken to from the cycling group the day before. "Hello again" he shouted as we approached, "you seen my group coming through? They should have been here ages ago". He seemed slightly worried. I told him that we hadn't seen anyone since leaving the café in the morning.

He had some boxes of assorted fruits and snacks ready for the group to arrive. "Help yourselves. We've got loads!" Being greedy and needing all the energy we could get, we took a couple of pieces of fruit each, before heading onwards with a vague promise to meet up in the pub later on.

We soon joined the tarmac for the short, but surprisingly steep final section of the days ride and into Tomintoul.

We were staying in the youth hostel ('The Smuggler's hostel'). We found it on the main street, and after discovering there was a shed we could lock our bikes inside, we dumped our stuff in the dorms. Nothing much was happening, so we went off to the pub in the square where we had some lovely food. We never did see the other group of cyclists that night (I imagine they were in some fancy hotel, living a life of luxury....what with their baths, complimentary soap, and private rooms).

And so we headed for bed. I was exhausted.

"ZZZZ-ZZZ-ZzZz-ZZzzz-hngGGggh-Ppbhww-zZZzzZZphhGG".......someone was snoring. After waiting some time hoping the culprit would turn over.....or just suffocate himself. I gave up and went to the shared living room/kitchen area only to find the sofa already occupied and two others asleep on the floor. Also...Sara was here, leaning against a counter top eyes half closed drinking a glass of water. I muttered "This is awful!".....she replied "well you booked it!". There should be a law against snoring in public...this man was stealing our sleep. I wandered back to the dorm hoping someone had killed the man busy sawing wood....the man's bunkmate rattled his bed until he awoke, apologised, moved around a bit, then resumed his snoring. A pillow flew across the room and stopped him for about five seconds.

Day 5: Tomintoul – Braemar

In the morning, it would be fair to say we were both grumpy. In fact everyone in the hostel was!......well......almost everyone.

As I sat outside sorting my stuff out so we could get out of here an old bearded man started talking. He asked where we were heading and then said we should keep an eye out as he'd seen a badger the previous day while walking along the same route.
He then told me a story about how one of his friends had a dog with no nose.....so I nodded and followed the accepted procedure: "oh....ok...how does it smell?" I asked........he then replied "no, no.....it was bitten off by a badger!!....vicious buggers."

We hit the tarmac. At the end of the street I turned the corner and felt the back end of the bike slipping slightly sideways. A sure sign of a deflating tyre. Before we'd even left the town I had my first puncture. I stopped, unhooked the panniers and upended my bike. Rather than waste time, I checked the tyre for thorns and glass before swapping out the inner tube for a fresh one. I'd fix the leaking tube later, somewhere more comfortable. Job quickly done, we wearily resumed cycling. Not the best way to start a day after a long sleepless night.

However, we were soon cycling down a beautiful valley and the smooth road made it very easy going. Then, where the OS map showed the tarmac running out, a freshly lain, perfectly smooth road continued. I was a bit disappointed as it didn't feel right to be going right into the heart of the hills on such a sanitised road.

We were soon disappointed further by a giant iron gate of the type you get in front of expensive mansions blocking the road. There didn't seem to be any way around. I checked the map. We must have made a mistake as this wasn't supposed to be here. It was like we wandered off into another dimension, a huge gate surrounded by mountains and trees. Why could this possibly be here? A secret military complex? A bear sanctuary? Was it to stop us getting in? Or was it protecting us from something? Perplexed, I pushed against the gates in case they were unlocked, nothing happened.

After checking the map, we did appear to be in the right place. There was a track off to the left which we considered taking but it looked like it didn't quite join back up with our intended route.

I slightly nervously pressed the buzzer on the gate. No-one answered. I waited and then pressed it again, this time I held the button for a while. Again no answer. Finally, it occurred to me that we should probably try the pedestrian gate off to one side. It pushed open. Weird. Through we went, and onwards, to whatever was awaiting us.

Soon after, at Inchrory, we passed a nice big house. There were no surprises awaiting us, no secret lairs, no bears.

A little further on and we came to some familiar territory. I'd cycled this part or the route several times in the opposite direction as part of the Loch Avon circular mountain bike route. One of my favourite overnight routes, with a great camping spot right by a loch right in the centre of the Cairngorms and miles from anywhere.

After a short time, we reached Loch Builg and the single-track path along the side. Knackered, we stopped by the loch to have a break. Stuffing our faces yet again, we saw a familiar looking group approaching along the loch. We'd stopped by a tough rocky section and so watched as every single rider cheerily said 'hello' and then failed to make it successfully down and over a small rock chute.

The group guide stopped for a chat and I asked about the earlier gate. I was told that the house we'd passed belonged to Madonna, and that she wasn't best pleased to find out about Scotland's right to roam laws which meant she couldn't stop people using the track (The Land Reform act of 2003 states the right to access most land and inland water providing you do so responsibly). Presumably the gate is enough to put plenty of people off from trying though!

I just looked it up while writing this, and it's now owned by the Sultan of Brunei. Hopefully, he's more accommodating to people crossing his land...though I doubt it.

The guide told me that one time he was guiding a group through and once through the gate was severely hassled by some people, presumably security people, telling him that he wasn't allowed to come through. The guide clearly knew his rights and told them to where to go. They were then closely followed all the way through the estate.

It was our turn to ride the rocky chute, we both failed to make it down. After the loch, the track split in two. We cycled down a brilliant hill for a couple of miles before I realised that something was wrong. "Errm....Sara....stop!" I shouted, "This doesn't look right." A quick look at the map was enough to see that, despite me having cycled this previously, we'd somehow taken a wrong turn. It was my fault as I'd been in front, and hadn't bothered to check the map at the junction. Back up the hill we had to go. Knowing that this climb was entirely unnecessary made it all the worse. We were, however, rewarded with seeing a large white mountain hare sprinting along the track though. He stopped a few metres from us. Then sprinted in a long circle right across the track around us on the other side, across the track again and back to the start. Maybe his burrow was at the edge of the road where we were standing, maybe he was trying to distract us. It's always nice to see some actual wildlife in the otherwise barren moorland maintained by the shooting estates.

After following the correct road for a few miles, we came the one monster climb of the day. Up the side of Culardoch, which topping out at 900m is a Corbett, the category of Scottish hills between 762 and 914 metres high or between 2,500 and 3,000 feet if you work in Imperial. Anything higher comes into the Munro category.

We live in a confused country, driving distances are measured in miles, cycling routes are measured in kilometres. I know I'm 6 foot 2, but have no idea what that is in cm even though I wouldn't measure anything else in feet. I've no idea how what 71 degrees Fahrenheit means, but know that I weigh about 12 stones. I'll order a pint of beer and buy a litre of milk. Petrol is also sold in litres but my car display tells me how many miles per gallon it's achieving.

Douglas Adams satirised this sorry state of affairs by coining the term 'sheppey', which is defined as the closest distance at which sheep remain picturesque. This is about 1.4km....or 7/8 miles. Another odd term is the 'Megafonzie' (Professor Farnsworth, Futurama), which is obviously a measure of an object's coolness.

Back on the hill, the track didn't go quite to the top, but it went far enough up. After the long struggle, where somehow I managed to keep going without stopping, I reached the high point of the road and wobbled from my bike to a conveniently placed rock for a rest. Nearby, a couple of hundred metres across the heather, was a small array of wire mesh boxes along with a weather station. This is an experiment site for the Macaulay Institute, an international centre for research on the environmental and social consequences of rural land uses. They are currently carrying out various climate change experiments, including testing the moorland to understand the impact of increased nitrogen deposits on the soil chemistry and local ecosystem. Pretty nice place to get to work!

We decided to stop for lunch and lay on jackets at the track side looking at the view while munching on sandwiches. Examining the map we could see it was mostly downhill all the way to our overnight stop in the town of Braemar. Ballater, a bit further along, would have made a better place to stop in terms of daily distance, but I couldn't find any accommodation for us. This meant that the following day would have to be a bit of a longer ride.

It was a beautiful afternoon. The heat of the sun making me sleepy as I lay back in the heather, looking at the sky, listening to the quiet buzz of nearby insects, and digested my Parma ham rolls.

Time to get on though, and down the steep hill we went. This was followed by an unexpected steep uphill again which I hadn't noticed on the map. From here on though, it really was downhill through some awesome countryside, into a forest, and all the way down to Invercauld house at the valley floor.

We then had a quick zoom along a very quiet tarmac road along a river's edge, crossed a bridge, and turned onto the main road before we cycled the few km of detour from the coast-to-coast route to reach Braemar. Soon we were enjoying some chips in the sunshine before heading to the Youth Hostel. Thankfully, nobody snored in my room this time.

Day 6: Braemar – Edzell

This was the longest day of the trip, about seventy kilometres, including a fair bit of road biking. The plan for the day ended with a tough climb over the last of the hills before the relative flat of the east coast.

It didn't start off too well. I woke early and was packing stuff into a pannier and thinking about breakfast when Sara appeared. "Dave....." she hesitated for a moment. "I'm done. I don't want go any further. I think we should stop somewhere until my flight back from Aberdeen". I was caught totally off guard, she'd seemed happy the day before. Certainly she hadn't appeared too tired. I didn't know how to respond. At first I thought she was maybe just coming down with a sudden cold or something. "What? Why? Are you feeling ill? Are you ok?"
"Noooo.....I'm just tired, I've had enough" she told me.
"Ok, lets get some breakfast and we'll decide what to do", I was trying to procrastinate for a bit in the hope that she'd change her mind. She seemed pretty sure, but I know what it's like when exhausted. Sometimes it's just a short term slump.

We went for breakfast at the Invercauld Arms, a big hotel in the centre of the town. Unfortunately, the greasy and yet frugal cooked breakfast wasn't up to much and did little to improve Sara's mood.

I persuaded her to keep going for a bit, thinking that she might be alright once she had a few miles under her wheels. The first bit of road was busy and tedious. Giant buses full of tourists passed too close on the tight corners. The cars seemed to be going too fast. "Great, this is all we need right now!" I thought to myself. Sara was slowly falling behind. I stopped and let her pass and cycle off in front, doing everything I could to prevent her from getting demoralised further. We finally reached Ballater after what seemed like a long ride and made out way into the centre of the small town.

I stopped and popped into a shop for some food and a coke. When I came out Sara told me that she really didn't want to go on. She'd had enough and had decided to stop. Maybe the rough tracks and climbs had taken their toll. Or maybe the lack of sleep from the two Youth Hostels.

I tried my best to persuade her to continue. I pointed out that this was basically the last day. Tomorrow was just a short easy ride to the beach. Not only that, but I knew that tonight's Bed & Breakfast would be good (judging solely by the price of the only place I could find!).

She started crying. I think she'd just had enough, maybe of me....maybe of sitting on the saddle for hours each day. I think she was just exhausted.

We looked at the bus stop, there were buses back to Aberdeen, and it wasn't too far. The bus would be along in an hour. We phoned and asked if they'd be able to take a bike and luggage on the bus and they said it would be no problem. I think Sara expected me to stop too. In retrospect maybe I should have, maybe I should have helped her back to Aberdeen and made sure she was ok and got the flight back in one piece. At that moment though, I was determined to finish the ride. I wasn't ready to stop.

She phoned a hostel in Aberdeen and made sure she'd have a place to stay. There didn't seem to be much else for me to do. I made a last attempt to persuade her to continue, but it came to nothing. We sat around for a bit...eating...passing the time until the bus. Finally it appeared and slowly made its way around the tight corners into the town square. "Well....this is it. Still time to change your mind?" I said. "Yep, I'm going. I'll call you" she replied. I gave her a hug, and waited until she was on the bus. I waved, and stood on the pavement for a few minutes. It looked like the bus was in no hurry to leave. So I did instead. It was already late and I had a long way to go.

The sun came out, and I hit the track road through the beautiful forest of Glen Tanar, south of Ballater. I felt terrible for Sara, but after the struggles of the morning it was good to be on my own for a bit. I could go at my own pace and it was great to just be enjoying the landscape I was travelling through, rather than worrying about my friend and having to stop all the time for her to catch up, or worrying that I'd gone too far ahead.

I knew I had a long way to go so I sped on, the smell of Scots pine in my nostrils and the needles crackling under the tyres.

Soon enough it was time to leave the forest and head along an exposed valley crossing a couple of wooden bridges and following the river. So far, so easy.

Now, already at an altitude of 350 metres, it was time to head higher...to 939 metres over the top of Mount Keen, a Munro. The track crossed the river for a last time and then headed away from the valley bottom and up the side of the mountain. The track wasn't too bad, even with all the weight on the back of the bike I was able to slowly work my way upwards. The views were great, the weather was great. What could go wrong?

The road turned into a nightmare. What had been a ride-able surface had become a rocky mess. Washed out by rainwater, the track turned to path, then a boulder filled ditch. Dragging my heavy bike up this wasn't much fun. I was able to push for a few metres before a big rock or hole would catch a wheel and force me to partially lift the bike past. Every time I had to put some extra power into a push, my feet would slide backwards on the gravelly surface. It was exhausting and frustrating. I made my way up slowly metre by metre. Soon, despite swapping to the other side of my bike, my lower back was aching from the effort.

Eventually though, I reached the top and lay in the heather breathing heavily from the exertion. This was the last hill of the trip. It had taken longer than I thought to get to the top, but I didn't care. It was sunny and warm....but mostly it was, from here on, downhill.

And a fun downhill too. I set off down the steep track, slowly sliding my way down the hill and over the rocks. On this bike I didn't have disc brakes, but instead the older style rim brakes. Part way down the hill the brakes blocks started to make a horrendous scraping noise. I stopped to take a look. They were almost completely worn out. Now I was worried they wouldn't last the distance and so had to take it easy as I continued my way downwards.

About half way down, the path turned into a better track road, which was more fun. Some switchbacks made things more interesting before the last smooth section down to the old buildings at the bottom on the valley floor. Phew, my brakes had held up. I was now in Glen Mark.

I stopped for a break at the Queen's well. Built 1861 in commemoration of Queen Victoria stopping for a drink......which is frankly a ridiculous reason. And people talk about how celebrity obsessed folks are nowadays!

If I'd felt energetic I could have tried to find the elusive Balnamoon's cave on the hillside nearby. Many people walk up this valley to search it out. Most return disappointed. The clandestine nature of the cave is the very reason it's famous.

In 1745, the supporters of the catholic King James (or 'Jacobus' in latin) were fighting to regain power from the incumbent southern protestants. These supporters, better known as the Jacobites, were beaten in a huge battle at Culloden by the Royal Army, led by the Duke of Cumberland (This is this is the same man who was in charge of the Ruthven barracks we visited back on day 4). Following the battle, the remaining Jacobite leaders split up and fled. James Carnegy, the 6th Earl of Balnamoon, escaped to Glen Esk where at first he hid in Invermark castle. However, with the royal army closing in and searching for him, the Earl needed to find somewhere less conspicuous to hide. He spent days searching the nearby hills until he found the small cave. To both hide it further and protect it from the elements he build a wall of stone and vegetation at the entrance-way. He hid, in the presumably pretty uncomfortable tiny cave, on-and-off for a year, until a local church minister gave him away and he was captured. This wasn't quite the end of his story though, as although the captured Jacobites were generally executed, there was some confusion over his identity and he was pardoned and released by mistake. The cave is today still nearly invisible. Only the most determined (or those who've been passed GPS co-ordinates) can find it.

I soon headed off down the sparsely populated Glen Esk, apparently the longest glen in Scotland. The track headed down past the Invermark Lodge and the nearby remains of the castle which was actually just a solid stone tower built in 1526. The track now turned to tarmac. From here it was a gentle roll down the quiet road. First I passed a place amusingly called 'Hole', and then a little later I passed 'Waggles'.

Nearing Edzell, and my stop for the night, I realised that although I only had a few miles to go it was only 4 o'clock. The earliest I'd finished all week despite the extra distance from Braemar and the long stop to see Sara off in Ballater.

I took a small detour along the edge of a gorge marked on the map as the 'rocks of solitude'. It was a fantastic little spot with the deciduous woods and the copper coloured river flowing down below and over some dramatic little falls. Apparently, this is great place to see salmon as they leap their way upstream, but I didn't see any although I stopped for a while to watch. Part of the way along the wooded paths I came across an old suspension bridge, which although all the main structure had gone, still had an intact but fragile looking metal and wire framework crossing to the other side of the gorge. I didn't dare test it. Finally I emerged from the path via an odd blue door in a wall, and was suddenly back on the road.

A short cycle down the road and I reached Edzell, a sizeable village with a few hotels and shops. It was here I was staying for the night.

I cycled around the back roads of the town for a bit, probably with a look of confusion on my face, until I eventually found the B&B I was staying at. It looked nice. Maybe a bit too nice for a cyclist after a week of not washing my clothes?

Worried about the state I was in, muddy, sweaty and slightly damp, I brushed myself down and rang the front door bell. It was opened by the owner who introduced herself as Elaine. She thankfully wasn't all perturbed by the mess that was about to enter her nice house. First, though, I took my bike around the side of the house to a garage where it could safely spend the night.

Trying to keep the mess to a minimum before being shown to my room, I removed my muddy shoes and padded across the thick carpet. Almost as soon I'd closed the door behind me, I stripped off and jumped straight into the hot shower.

All clean, I headed out for a walk and met the same group of mountain bikers that I'd kept bumping into, in the pub. We chatted about the massive hill from earlier and how much they'd enjoyed the trip and how great the ride was. Although they were clearly slightly inebriated, I had to agree.

After getting some pub food, and maybe a couple of pints, I said my goodbyes and headed back to a very comfy bed.

Day 7: Edzell to Montrose

I slept very well, and got up at the allotted time for breakfast. There was one other guest. An old bearded New-Zealander called Terry who was over to visit his family. While we waited for our full-cooked breakfasts to arrive we chatted about Aberdeenshire as he'd been further up north for a visit and that's where I was brought up. He seemed to be enjoying himself and kept saying that it had changed a lot since he was last over.

He asked about my trip and told me about how he used to cycle a lot when he was younger, although he'd never gone on a long trip. And as he had a couple of days to spare I gave him some suggestions on a couple places he could visit.

Our breakfasts arrived and silence fell upon the room as we hungrily devoured the lot and drank coffee. Terry wanted to see my bike, I think he was interested to see how much stuff I was carrying for a week. So after getting the key off the owner we went out to the garage to take a look.

I had my second puncture. The back tyre was completely flat. Terry gave me a hand to remove the panniers, lifting them up and down to get an idea of the weight before saying "Christ!.....that's some weight to be dragging about". I agreed and emptied out a load of stuff I hadn't used even once on the trip, in order to get to a spare inner tube.

Finally, ready to go, I said goodbye to everyone and headed off. Today was road all the way, but it was only 25 kilometres to the coastal town of Montrose.

It was entirely uneventful. A surprising and unexpected hill was overcome and then around lunch time I rolled into town. It was much like any other market town, full of pleasant enough shops and a bit dreary. I cycled up the high street which had some nice buildings; a large town hall with an arched area under the front, an old church and a red sandstone library. Maybe I was just feeling a bit down at my trip ending, but I was thinking that this was a terrible, depressing place to end the trip. Maybe if I'd have known a bit more about its history I'd have appreciated a bit more at the time.

A settlement has been here since prehistoric times. It was later attacked multiple times by the Danish, who took everything worth stealing before finally adding insult to injury by burning the whole place to the ground in 980. It was rebuilt and became an important trading town. Then, in 1244....it was burnt to the ground again. Only to be rebuilt, again. A castle was built in 1178 by William the Lion. Another castle was built to house an English garrison and was destroyed by William Wallace who apparently killed every soldier on sight (presumably not single-handedly although this isn't reported).

In the 15th century the town was again plundered, this time by some rich Lairds with a multitude of heavy weapons. Before King James the 4th (not the Jacobite one, that was the 7th) Sorted them out.

The town really took off in the 17th century as a major trading port, mostly dealing with hides, smoked salmon, and grains before getting into the wine trading business with imports coming from France and Portugal. In the course of the next century, it became a big smuggling port and to its shame, became involved in slave trading. By now it was a hugely affluent town. Later, it was an important base during the second world war, hosting both squadrons on Hurricanes and Spitfires as well as becoming a military port.

A large St Bernard dog named "Bamse", which means 'teddy bear' in Norwegian arrived on a Norwegian minesweeper. He was a registered crew member and became famous for stopping fights as well as saving at least one life. He died in Montrose docks and the schools were closed for his funeral where he was afforded a precession with all 800 children lining the streets.

If I'd know any of this at the time I might have been inspired to take a better look around. I might have come across the statue of Bamse which has been erected on the dock and given him a pat. As it was, I wasn't aware, and nothing about the town hinted at it's past.

I wanted to get to the actual coast seeing as I was doing the coast-to-coast route, so I looked at a handy signpost with a map of the town on it and figured out a route to the beach. But before making my way to the sea, I bought some cherry bakewells and then checked the small train station to figure out when the next train out of here was. Now I was at the end, I was keen to get out of here. There wasn't a timetable, so I asked at the ticket office when the next train to Edinburgh was. "three hours time" the man grumpily told me. "What?!?" this town had nothing of interest in it. Three hours!

As I left the station as was cycling back along the side with a fence between me and the platform, a train came in...it had a sign on the door that clearly read "Edinburgh", what the hell! I span around, but it had already started moving again before I got back to the station. I thought about complaining to the ticket office man, but it seemed pointless. He'd clearly given up caring years ago.

I headed down to the seafront where I surprisingly, and for the final time, met the cycling group again. After a bit of chat and they asked if I wanted a lift, of course I did! Unfortunately, it turned out they were going the wrong way. Still, it was brilliant to meet them at the end after meeting the whole way across and sharing at least parts of the same experience.

I said goodbye and headed down to the beach and as the weather was now getting worse, I sheltered in between some sand dunes and ate all six cherry bakewells.

It started to rain. I decided to head back to the station and, surprise, a train arrived. I got on it. It wasn't going to Edinburgh, but I didn't care. It was stopping half-way. I hoped to switch at a busier station to get an onwards train. It was time to go home.

51

Capital Trail route:

Capital Trail

I spotted the first mention of the Capital Trail on twitter. An intriguing looking picture of a mountain bike in the wilderness, loaded up with bike-packing equipment popped up, with a short description of a new event based in my home city, Edinburgh. I clicked the accompanying link.

A website for the yearly local cycle festival opened up. I'd heard a lot about the festival over the years, and I'd previously looked at the website. It had all sorts of interesting stuff on there, tours around the cycle paths of Edinburgh, courses for commuters, cycling fashion shows and bike maintenance course. All of which are great, but I'd rather just go out for a cycle on my own. I've never really been a big fan of organised fun.

This time however, the page opened showing a map of a route starting on the beach not far from my house and stretching for 237 kilometres while incorporating many of my local mountain bike routes.

It looked awesome. Set up as a time trial format (although technically it wasn't a race) the aim was to complete it in 40 hours or less. I thought about it and figured that, for me at least, it looked like a crazy amount of biking in such a short time. The Capital Trail route took in about six or seven of the routes that would normally each occupy me for an afternoon. To do all of those in two days, as well as the connections between, while carrying enough equipment and food for an overnight stop seemed impossible. I looked further and saw that there was over 6000m of climbing.

Obviously, I clicked the apply button and filled in the short application form. Apparently, only 100 people were going to be allowed to take part in the inaugural ride and I thought I probably didn't have to worry about the distance as I most likely wouldn't be picked to be one of them.

The email arrived, I was surprised not to see a rejection message, and henceforth my adventure was seemingly unavoidable.

I paid the small entry fee.

Later I told my girlfriend that I'd be away mountain biking for another weekend. She looked at me with her "go to bed" eyes. I joined the Facebook group created for the event, and was glad to spot a few familiar faces, including a French guy called Remy who I'd met once in the middle of the Cairngorms during a horrible, cold and windy day.

I had been following a very remote route, cycling along an elevated and exposed track road miles from anywhere, when he came flying down another steep track from the top of a hill. He was surprised to see anyone else out here. We had a quick chat (it was too cold to stop for long) which started with him saying something like "it's freezing up there and I had to lean over at about 45 degrees into the wind....horrible". He said 'good luck!', then headed off down the better main track. When working out the route on a map earlier, I'd also planned to go right to the top of the hill, so I headed up. He wasn't wrong about the wind and the horribleness, but it was a lot of fun coming back down.

I met him a bit later again after he'd taken a wrong turn allowing me to catch up. We chatted while we cycled back out of the hills together. As we passed a remote house a friendly young dog sprinted out from behind a fence and ran along beside us. We crossed a sheep grid, thinking he'd stop. But he pushed through a gap in the fence at the side and quickly caught up. He didn't seem to be giving up, so we floored it and sprinted as hard as we could. When I turned around, the dog was still there. We split up, hoping that it would get confused and we'd lose it. But he was too cunning. We were now quite a distance from his home and he was still following. Giving up, and not wanting a new pet, we decided we had no option but to turn back and return the dog to its owners. Luckily after a few miles, and in a cloud of dust, a 4x4 appeared up the track. The owners had come to find him and gratefully scooped him into the back with a "thank you guys!"

I've been bike-packing many times before, but never on a time-trial. My usual equipment would be to mount a single pannier, use a backpack and take my light 1kg tent, sleeping bag, ground mat, stove, food and tools. It all added up to a fair amount of extra weight and no doubt slowed me down and tired me out. It had worked well enough for me though, and had enabled many overnight trips through the Cairngorm mountains or the hills of Dumfries-shire.

I needed to be lighter this time though if I was going to stand any chance of making the distance.

The most obvious place to save weight was to do away with the pannier and rack.

You'd think doing outdoor activities would be an escape from modern life. A break from the daily grind of adverts, rampant commercialism and the constant pressure to have new stuff. The hounding of the human soul by being constantly told to buy, buy buy. From pre-packaged, auto-tuned, voice warbling, talent show winning stars who are going to be huge, to new super-foods, everything is cynically marketed to make you spend your hard earned money.

The outdoor activity market is as bad as the worst of them. And I for one have had enough!

I spent hours online navigating the various options before ordering a saddle pack, and a new brightly coloured sleeping mat...

The saddle pack straps on to both the seat post and the bottom of the saddle, and hangs out the back of the bike rider like a bee's abdomen. Into this pack I could fit a sleeping bag, food and tools. The positioning of this weight surprisingly also didn't affect the handling of the bike too much. It's certainly a lot lighter than the pannier equivalent for the same carrying load.

I was also advised to swap my tent for a bivy bag. This is a fairly simple thick waterproof, sometimes breathable, bag which you surround your sleeping bag with while you are sleeping.....on the ground.....with no other cover...and usually while midges attack your head. This is a popular option with bike-packers. I opted instead to stick with the relative comfort of my small tent, despite the extra weight.

I didn't have a dedicated GPS, so I installed an app on my phone which I hoped would do the job instead, hopefully saving the time and hassle of looking at maps.

I had to test it all out before the start of the event, so I choose a nice evening and set off for the Pentlands, the hills just on the edge of Edinburgh. I hung around my house procrastinating for far too long before I finally set off.

I headed out of town, staying away from the busy roads by making use of the canal, passing over a viaduct on its perilously thin, cobbled path. I've had few problems while crossing, but have heard many stories of conflict between people trying to cross in opposite directions. These include a suited cyclist in his fifties trying to force his way rudely past a pedestrian also in his fifties, who responded by putting him in a headlock and trying to throw him into the canal. I also overheard a one-eyed man shouting at a jogger and calling him a 'baldy c***' before turning and by way of explanation saying 'I'm disabled, I've got that many broken bones'.

A couple of hours of cycling later it was getting seriously dark. I had a head torch and used it for the last hour up a rocky track, sheep eyes glowing as I passed, climbing higher. Eventually, after looking and failing to find a good spot to camp a couple of times, I neared the spot I'd seen on an earlier outing. Unfortunately, actually getting to the camping spot involved climbing up a 100m high, steep, rocky hillside. No easy task in the dark while carrying a bike. Anyway, I made it, and hurriedly set about erecting my tiny tent in the strong wind doing my best to peg it down before it blew away. Climbing into my sleeping bag never felt so good. I watched the moving lights of cars on a distant road as I heated up some packet soup as a reward. Even cold and tired, the powdered soup was still a disappointment. I'll never learn.

The wind howling around the tent did nothing to stop me falling asleep on my new, but slightly more squeaky than hoped, lightweight air mattress.

I awoke at four, needing a pee. As I stumbled out into the freezing air and let loose, I looked up to see an amazing sun-rise. The sky was a fiery red and orange and as I stood shivering, the sky noticeably brightened. Job done, I climbed back into the comfort and warmth. I wish I'd thought to take a photo of the view.

Waking early, I opened the tent door and looked out at the view for a while before working up the energy to lean over to the stove and boil some water for coffee and porridge.

My feet were cold and wet for some reason. I'm quite tall and my feet had been pressing on the bottom of the tent allowing my sleeping bag to slowly absorb the moisture/condensation. I made a mental note to stick a waterproof bag over the end of my sleeping bag next time.

Fully awake and dressed, I carefully packed up the tent and reattached everything to my bike. Heading back towards home the sun came out. I took my time, choosing a route which had the most fun bits of single-track. It was a beautiful sunny morning. The test-ride was complete.

I'd learnt a few things on my test ride. There were quite a few things I didn't need to carry, the phone GPS app I was using to navigate was fine for short trips but used up too much battery for longer trips, and I would have had to buy a water proof case and mount to attach it to my handlebars for it to be really useful. I endeavoured to buy a very cheap GPS on ebay.

The day of the race finally arrived. I slowly rode the couple of miles from my house down to the beach. It was a perfect day for cycling. The couple of days before had been some of the hottest days of the summer. Hot enough to dry out muddy paths, probably too hot to be comfortable for a long ride.

Registering at the Tide café, I got myself an unexpected free second breakfast of a cup of tea and bacon roll and chatted to a few familiar faces. Most people were comparing bikes and how much stuff everyone else was carrying. I seemed to be somewhere at the heavier end of the scale. One guy had previously posted a photo of his bike to the Capital Trail website. The image showed he had nothing on his bike but for a tiny bag attached under his saddle. It looked about big enough to hold his keys, although apparently there was a bivy bag in there. I had thought the photo was a joke, but here he was without even a backpack.

I wondered about if I could ditch anything, but honestly apart from a really lightweight lock I'd brought along there was nothing which didn't seem essential to my ride.

There was good mix of standard mountain bikes, single-speeds (everything kept simple for reliability), and a good number of fat-bikes. These last are serious adventure bikes originally invented for winter riding in Alaska. They have oversized tyres for bump absorption, grip, and to prevent sinking into soft terrain. It was getting close to the start time of 8am, when we were all ushered down onto the sandy beach for the mass start. It was quite a sight to see the long line of bikes stretched out across the beach. A few photos were taken. I felt that at any moment a director would appear shouting 'cut'. The scene was odd. It didn't feel real. Then, someone sprinted out of the pack and shouted go, and we were off. A sedate roll down the promenade followed. I spent a minute going slow, pressing buttons on my new GPS until the route appeared.

The route tested everyone's navigational skills almost immediately by twisting through woods and along overgrown river paths as it led us out of the city. I chatted to some others about whether they had done this sort of ride before. They mostly asked me why I was wearing knee pads (to protect my broken knee from the year earlier!).

Soon enough we reached the countryside proper and after crossing several fields and a road section, it was time for the first proper hill. The pack was spreading out. Already some sections were too steep to cycle up. I tried my best to make it to the top but didn't quite have the gears to make it with the extra weight. The pushing had begun.

At the top was a wonderful undulating section with views of the nearby wind turbines and reservoir. The track zig-zagged, descending the other side of the hill and past a bothy. Just next to which was the first of many water crossings. I nervously pointed my front wheel into the water and rode through. It wasn't too deep and was fine to cycle through either with care, or just speed. As I climbed the steep track on the other side of the valley, I heard a yelp and some laughing. I turned to see someone who'd toppled off of their bike and while they were not quite submerged completely, they clearly were getting a good soaking.

After the second hill and we were already passing Bunny's bothy, a small cabin, sometimes open for public use and the first suggested overnighting point. We were now about a third of the way in terms of distance. So far, so good. The riding hadn't been too difficult....yet. I was pretty happy with my progress. I could definitely feel the distance in my legs, but felt like they had plenty left to give.

Some more descents and a road section and I arrived in the town of Lauder. A couple of riders were cycling away from the route. Presumably looking for supplies. I pushed through and on towards the nearby town of Melrose. A book festival was in full swing, which meant that it was busy.

As I wove my through the streets packed with cars and people, I spotted a few riders already sitting outside a café enjoying a break. I saw another helmet wearer standing outside a shop eating an ice cream. As I was carrying all my food, I didn't need to stop, and continued on past a herd of bikes sitting outside the co-op supermarket. Instead, I dropped down to a fast rolling path along the edge of the river.

Further on I stopped for lunch on the riverbank. A portion of granola with powdered milk in a sandwich bag, to which I only had to add water, an idea I'd read about on a bike-packing forum. It worked well. Powdered milk is so much better than that horrible long life stuff you get in hotels. After eating the milky meal I just had a damp bag to dispose of. Very efficient.

After 15 minutes of sitting, no-one had gone past. I was just beginning to wonder whether I'd taken a wrong turn, when a rider in a white top passed shouting "phew, this must be the right way

after all". Already, the route was spreading us out.
I packed my spork and mug and cycled after him.

I caught up with the cyclist who introduced himself as Andy. We cycled along through woods and along single track tarmac roads while he regaled me with tales of his past jobs, hobbies and cycling adventures. He said he recognised me from doing some previous mountain bike events. I don't think we'd ever talked though.

I realised I was almost out of water. Not quite sure when the next opportunity to refill would be, when we passed a small fast running river I decided to make the short detour. I was just about to head off down a track when Andy said that he thought we were about to go through Selkirk where I'd easily be able to fill up. Several confusing, twisty kilometres later, and a quick check of the GPS showed that instead of heading into town, we were now being directed into Yair forest. I was saved from a long waterless climb by a slightly muddy hose in the courtyard of a farm.

Up and up we climbed. The track getting steeper as we went. Eventually, legs feeling the effort, I reached the Three Brethren stone markers at the summit first. I lay my bike down and stuffed a cereal bar into my mouth. Sugary food never tasted better. Before I'd finished, Andy arrived. We sat leaning against the nearby trig point and stared out at the view in silence for ten minutes. I could see a couple of other cyclists in the distance working their way up the hill. I wondered how many were in front of us. I had no-idea how we were doing in terms of the race. "Let's go!" exclaimed Andy as he jumped to his feet.

We set of down and along the hill tops to Minch Moor and our first section of proper man-made mountain bike track.

I'd been down the Innerleithen red route many times before. But never with a heavy saddle pack. To be honest I was surprised by how little it changed the bike handling, but even so, after hopping off the first couple of little drop-offs on the route, I stuck to the chicken-runs avoiding any issues. It was still fun riding the berms and tabletops, albeit as a slower pace than usual. This bike-packing stuff was turning out great.

We were soon back on track roads as we rode for a long distance, skirting the hills around to the second suggested overnight spot at another bothy. It was still too early to consider stopping for the night, but we stopped for a break with some other cyclists. I sat in the long grass and broke out some tinned fish which, when scooped onto some bread made a great sandwich.

"What the hell are you eating?" asked Andy.

"Want some?" I replied, holding up the tin.

"No thanks.....you're alright!" he laughed and moved slightly further away.

The tin was wrapped in an empty bag and spent the remainder of the trip doing it's best to make my spare clothes smell terrible.

Down the last bit of hill and onto a road, we were joined by a bearded fellow biker. "Which way do we go now?" he asked. His GPS had run out of batteries. Not ideal. "Mind if I cycle along with you guys for a bit?" But seconds later he changed his mind after seeing the sign 'Innerleithen 1/2m'. "Actually, I'm going to go buy some more batteries.....See you later".

Andy and I continued on. For kilometres the cycling was relatively easy. We rode along quiet farm roads through lovely deciduous woods. It made a nice change from the uniform forestry pines that we had been seeing up until now. The early evening sun was glinting through the gaps in the trees as we passed intermittently from darkness into bright light and back again. At the literal end of the road we came to the last suggested spot for overnighting. It looked like a nice place to spend the night, but we were still up for more cycling. The onwards route took us towards a steep heather covered hillside with little in the way of obvious paths. The route instructions said this was where you just had to go up until you re-joined the route higher up. Following the exact GPS track for this section wasn't mandatory. We started pushing. The ground was soft, the heather and the steepness were doing their best to sap any remaining energy I had. I was again cursing the weight of my bike and equipment. The effort didn't seem to be effecting Andy. All the way up he was chatting away. I had to stop turn around and grumpily say 'what?' every time it sounded like he had asked a question as otherwise I couldn't actually hear what he was saying over my heavy breathing, grunting and the noise of the bike crushing the heather.

I knew we were looking for a track running across the side of the hill. For a long time I couldn't see it. And just as I thought I spotted it way further up, I suddenly realised it was right in front of me. Thank god. I dropped my bike to the ground and started to recover my breath. Andy arrived right behind and we, under the pretence of taking some photos, had a rest.

A combination of the height we'd just gained, climbing into the mist, and the time of day meant that it was getting rapidly colder. It was no time to be standing about. Onwards.

This track was cycle-able for a short distance, but soon it was steep enough that we were back to pushing. We persevered all the way to the fence at the top of the ridge between two hills. Once the other side of the fence, the track looked better. Looks can be deceiving. The rutted track soon got steeper and although I could probably have struggled up it, it seemed easier to get off and push. At least the surface meant it was much easier to roll the bike along. Finally....finally....I spotted the big cairn at the very top of the hill appearing through the mist. This was Birkscairn hill, the highest point of the whole trip at a 661 metres. We didn't stop to celebrate.

From here it was a long and fast downhill along the hilltops along the edge of the Gypsy Glen. Andy set of in front and quickly disappeared off into the distance as I carefully negotiated the ruts and drops and rocks. Some way down I caught up. His bike was ominously upended. A puncture.

I may be paraphrasing, but he said something like "Go on without me, I'll only slow you down". Being a good soldier, I said he'd probably only be five minutes and I'd wait. I then gallantly sat down next to a wall glad of the rest. I didn't offer much help.

Andy pulled a large spike out of his tyre. It was organic, but didn't look like it had come from a plant. We decided it might be a hedgehog spine. Maybe some kind of revenge for hedgehog brethren who had been run over by cars.

"Fuck....I'm such an idiot", Andy was holding two inner tubes and looking annoyed. The spare tubes had the fatter Schrader valves. The wheel rims on his bike only had holes big enough for the smaller Presta type of valve.

I mentioned that I had a Presta valved spare in my saddle-bag. But after examining my rims, I also couldn't have used the bigger spares. If I gave Andy my spare, I wouldn't be able to get another, given the time of night. If I'd then had a puncture, that would have been it for me for the race. Game over. We were about one kilometre from Peebles. The only option was for Andy to walk down and wait there until the morning to buy a new spare.

I felt bad, but I had to go. Maybe I should have given him my spare, but I reasoned that I wouldn't want anyone else to give me their only spare if I thought they would have had a chance of needing it in the middle of nowhere. At least, that's how I legitimised my selfishness.

I set off and rolled down an awesome path which swooped and twisted its way smoothly downwards. I thought I was going fast, but still a couple of people overtook me. As I stopped to open a pedestrian gate, I heard a shout from behind "open itttt!". Someone, was skidding towards the gate far too fast, their brakes locking up their back wheel. I slammed the gate open and they safely passed though. "Cheeeeerrrrsss!" I continued down an equally fun, grassy path towards the town of Peebles and after getting some more water at a stream made my way into the town. I crossed an old Victorian pedestrian bridge. Suddenly four or five other mountain bikers appeared behind me. We stopped for a moment to figure out which way to go (the GPS route does a figure of eight here and it was important to go the right way around the loops, which I couldn't easily tell from the screen).

Confident that I knew which way to go I set off, followed by several of the other bikers.

"This isn't right, we need to go the other way" one said.

"Aye, this is heading out of Peebles" agreed another.

"Yeah, that's where I'm going....Glentress!" I said.

They grumbled and turned back, except for one, the bearded guy from earlier who'd needed batteries for his GPS.

"I'm doing Glentress as well....then back for chips!" he grinned. We set off.

As we climbed the steep hill to the upper car park of the Glentress mountain bike trail centre I found out his name was Jay. He and I chatted about all sorts. He has a daughter the same age as mine. So we talked about the crazy things kids of that age get up to. He was good company and we seemed to be fairly well matched in terms of speed. Once on the red/blue graded mountain bike route that we were following, it all seemed easy compared to some of the earlier riding. This was relatively smooth and designed to be cycle-able. I even managed to get some air over the jumps on the way down through 'spooky woods'. The light was beginning to fade as we made our way down through the last sections of forest, making it tricky to do much more than aim the bike towards the bits that weren't trees. We made it out at the bottom and thought it was going to be an easy ride along the road back to Peebles. Jay had convinced me to stop with him at the fish and chip shop. However, looking at the GPS, it was clear we were off to one side of the marked route and going straight instead of wiggling about. We rode back to the start and found a small path leading into a very dark wood. This was presumably what we were supposed to be following.

Cycling through the trees, it was very dark. If the lure of chips hadn't been so strong, I'd have stopped and dug out my head torch, but as it was, I literally ploughed on through the undergrowth, bumping over roots and rocks. This was much slower than the road, and hard work.

Eventually we burst out of the darkness and onto a sports field. A short ride took us into the centre of town and the chip shop. Some large orders were made.

Soon some other cyclists arrived and we chatted about the ride while stuffing ourselves and drinking sugary drinks. Most were planning to stop in Peebles for the night and do the Glentress route in the morning. At least it looked like we weren't going to be last! A couple of them had just finished the Glentress route, although they were also done for the day. Two guys were trying to book a hotel for the night...they were exhausted and looking for some comfort.

Full up, Jay and I cycled out of town. It was almost midnight and properly dark now. Head-torches were dug out and deployed. We planned to stop at the first decent spot we could find for some sleep. Of course the ride out of town was up a steep hill. I struggled up it, I really needed to just stop cycling now. I'd pretty much been riding for sixteen hours, with the longest break being twenty minutes in the chip shop. Near the top of the hill, and behind a wall we found a sheltered spot in a small wood where the trees were black and motionless.

I was so happy to be off my bike. I set up my tent and spent ten minutes blowing up my lightweight air mattress, an endurance event of its own. Throwing everything into my tent I said goodnight as Jay climbed into his bivy bag. Laying down was never more comfortable. Just being still for a while and stretching out fully felt great. As a nearby owl hooted loudly, I thought about the day's adventure. I was exhausted, but really enjoying it. I'm not sure if I had adrenalin running through my veins, or just the excitement of the day, but I couldn't get to sleep. It didn't matter. Resting was enough.

I woke and looked at my watch, it was 2am, and still dark. I'd somehow slept for almost two hours. After a while I heard a terrifying screeching coming from somewhere near my tent. I presumed it was coming from the owl rather than Jay. I shuffled about and dozed for a while, with no intention of getting up.

"Dave........Dave........DAVE.......DAAAVE......are you awake?" Jay was awake.
"yeah...I'm awake."
"Do you fancy making a move?"

65

It was still dark, but I felt ready to go. "Ok...lets do it!". It was almost 3am.

I quickly packed and although I wasn't hungry I ate a cereal bar and opened up a packet of cheesy oatcakes to share. Jay had survived in his bivy, he reported that he didn't even think there were any midges about. I asked if he'd heard the screeching. "What screeching?" he'd slept right through it....or maybe he was hiding something?

Within ten minutes of getting out of bed, we were finding our way by torchlight back out of the woods and onto the track. Luckily we'd done the worst of the climb the night before and now had a relatively easy start crossing fields and following footpaths. As it slowly got lighter, we plodded along almost in silence. I was enjoying being up at this hour. I felt pretty great for having only had a couple of hours sleep. My legs felt good and my sore back from the previous day had gone. Hopes for a beautiful sunrise were dashed when it became evident how cloudy and misty it was. Still, it was a great time to be up. We pushed our bikes up a steep wide path into a pretty pine forest to the immense sound of birds singing all around.

A quick descent was followed by a long climb up the side of a grassy valley and then back into more forest. Eventually, we emerged onto the road at West Linton and cycled into the town. It was now shortly after 5am. Jay was talking about buying a coffee. I pointed out that given the time and it being a Sunday morning in a tiny town, he was being just slightly optimistic. He was still disappointed as we passed the closed paper shop where he'd hoped there'd be a coffee machine. As we rode on we joked about breaking into someone's house, or knocking on a door. I think we were possibly losing it.

We had to climb another steep track out the back of West Linton, but once that was out of the way, it was a gentle uphill for several miles along very bumpy track until we reached Carlops. We were getting close to Edinburgh again. From here I knew the tracks well, and I was dreading the next section.

A couple of kilometres later and we reached nine-mile burn,

I had tried and failed to cycle in this direction before. Even with an unladen bike I hadn't managed to cycle up the next hill, Cap Law, and had even struggled with the push. I'd learnt a lesson that the circular day routes through the Pentland hills which involved this section should definitely only be done in one direction. The Capital Trail, not lacking a challenge or two, routed us up this terrible hill in the other direction.

I was tired, it was misty, and starting to rain heavily when we started the climb. I knew the wind, from which we'd been fairly sheltered until this point, was going to be strong and in our faces. Onwards we pushed. I had to lift my bike and luggage over three unavoidable fences. My back was now aching again. Every lift took everything I had just to scrape the bike over the barbed wire. We trudged upwards. It was getting colder, and the rain was getting heavier. The higher we climbed the stronger the wind got. I managed to pedal over a few of the flatter sections. Forcing the wheels of the bike onwards through the boggy ground. Jay was forging ahead, while I wasn't far behind. We didn't speak for the whole climb. Just when I thought we'd reached the top, I could see that the hill kicked up steeply again. There was no option but to accept the atrocious situation and just keep on going.

Finally, the path led off to the right and skirted the rounded summit. This was no time to celebrate. The weather was getting worse. We cycled on until finally we lost some height and at a stile stopped for a moment. Jay was shaking from the cold, I was more exhausted than I ever remember being. Still, the next section was mostly downhill, hopefully getting us out of the wind.

We stopped at the bottom while Jay put on every bit of clothing he possessed. I was glad of the rest and took my gloves off to eat an energy bar. By now my 'waterproof' gloves were so wet that putting them on was a real struggle. I couldn't get all my fingers in. I considered not wearing them, but instead opted to cycle on like a cliché of a comedian doctor who can't put his latex gloves on properly.

The next section was a relief. Through the valley in the middle of the Pentland hills. Followed by a steep, but straight forwards climb back out over the hills to the Edinburgh side. From here we practically rolled down and into Edinburgh. The route taking us along the canal right in the centre, before diverting down the cobbled tourist destination of the Royal Mile.

There was still a last sting in the tail of the route. Just as we were thinking it might be an easy roll back down to the finish at the beach, the route took a hard right, and the road veered upwards once again. We slowly climbed up, around the edge of Arthur's Seat, a large, volcanic, hill near the city centre. Every time I thought the road would flatten, we'd take another turn and head upwards again. We were directed onto a footpath, which, surprisingly, went upwards, until finally, we'd reached the top. A left turn and a fast descent through some trees and across a park and we were rewarded with an amazing view of the coast stretching from the Forth bridges in the west to the power-station and Bass Rock in the east. Best of all, right in front of us was the finish.

We rolled downhill, and along a section of old railway for a few kilometres, to the top of a long road. Right at the other end of the road, at the bottom of the hill, was the beach. "It's too easy" I said. "I bet the route cuts off to the right, up a massive hill". Luckily I was wrong, we hit Portobello promenade, where we'd started the cycle 240 kilometres ago.

The finish was at the Tide Café where we'd started, and so we still had a kilometre or so to go. For some reason I said to Jay "We should have a sprint for the finish?" Gallantly he replied "nah, I think we should finish together". I should have left it there, but said it'd be a fun way to finish. He grinned and agreed. As soon as the café came into sight, I floored it. Inevitably, he quickly passed me and shot off into the distance. I arrived at the café about thirty seconds behind. It was 9:15 am.

Markus met us outside the café and heated up some very welcome coffee in his parked car. We were surprised to learn that we were about 15th. An excellent result. I thought we were much further back. Our total time was 25 hours and 15 minutes.

I asked the time of the winner. "15 hours" replied Markus.

An incredible time. 10 hours faster!

However, we'd timed it almost to perfection. The café opened a few minute later, and we ordered full breakfasts and coffee.

Mull Route:

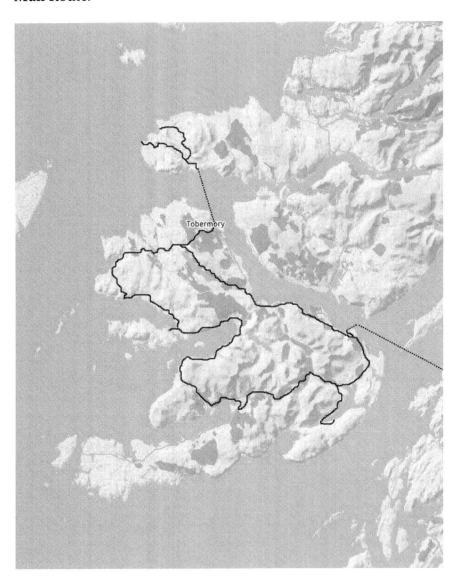

Mull

Soon I was looking for more cycling adventures. I met up with a friend, Al, whom I've known since I was 4, and he suggested taking a few days off to do a cycle of some sort.

When I was younger we lived in the north-east of Scotland in Aberdeenshire, farming and forestry country. My parents were friends with the couple who lived in the old Manse not far from my house. The house was a huge four story built in 1821 to house the local minister. My folks would often go visit and play war based board games. In fact my mum soon dreaded being asked over for dinner as she found the games incredibly boring. The house was huge, had a cold, almost medieval, basement and expansive gardens and outbuildings.

The couple moved out and Al and his family moved in. My parents took me to visit. I was jealous of him living in that house.

One of my fist memories of him is of being on the primary school bus and Al convincing me that both his and my parents had agreed for me to come to his house to play, which of course they hadn't. Later, after some frantic phone calls my mum arrived to angrily take me home.

As one of my closest neighbours (I lived about a mile away), we'd often cycle to each other's houses or spend the long summer days cycling about the quiet roads and getting up to mischief.

Al also seems fairly accident prone. The first one I remember is when we were descending a tree using the barbed wire fence at the bottom as an extra foothold. He somehow fell back, the barbs caught on the back of his thigh and ripped a hole in his leg. I also remember him smashing a tooth or two while jumping a gap in a wall and crashing bikes many times. This bad luck seems to have continued into adulthood. Somehow, he is still mostly in one piece.

Al suggested going to the west coast somewhere, possibly a route taking in an island. Looking at a map of Scotland, Mull looked like a good bet, it's the second largest of the Western Isles (excepting the distant Outer Hebrides), with only Skye being larger. So with its almost 300 mile long coastline it was certainly big enough to spend a few days cycling around.

Although I'd previously been camping on the east side of it for a couple of nights and taken a bus up to Tobermory at the north end, I hadn't really explored much. I was keen to go back, camping there with my girlfriend had been great. We'd woken one morning at our seaside camp-site and opened the tent door to see a big pod of dolphins, seemingly playing and jumping out of the water, not far away.

In anticipation of the cycle trip, I started reading up on the island.

Mull is thought to have been first inhabited shortly after the ice receded north, around 6000BC. There is lots of evidence supporting this, including brochs, stone circles, burial cairns, standing stones and plenty of pottery. It sounded like there'd be plenty of interesting remains to explore on a bike ride.

It's thought than Christianity was first brought to Scotland by a monk, St Columba, who came across from Ireland and set up a monastery on the small Island of Iona, just off to the south-west of Mull.

During WWII the whole island was restricted, Tobermory being used as a training base "HMS Western Isles" for anti-submarine techniques for the crews of the Atlantic convoy escorts. The base was run by Vice Admiral Gilbert Stephenson. He was a bit of an eccentric, firing people on a whim if he thought they weren't up to scratch and famously, during a routine inspection, he threw down his hat and declared it 'a bomb'. A low ranking trainee quickly kicked it into the sea and was commended for his quick thinking. The commander then declared his hat 'a man overboard' and the trainee had to jump into the freezing sea to retrieve it.

The island only has about 3000 inhabitants, although it can get busy with tourists during the summer.

I was hoping to see some of the reportedly varied wildlife, possibly golden and sea eagles, or even better; basking sharks or minke whales, neither of which I've ever seen. Many, many times I've excitedly taken photos of distant fins moving through the water. Only to examine them later on a computer screen, zooming in, comparing the shapes of the curve at the back of the fins, to find out they were dolphins. Don't get me wrong, these are still nice to see, but are a fairly common sight around the coasts of Scotland.

This time we were going to be on the road the whole way. And we planned to camp the whole way. Scotland's amazing access legislation called 'the Land Reform act (2003)' allows anyone to legally camp on almost any land as long as it's done responsibly. The main idea is to not disturb and leave no trace. And for the most part it's brilliant. As always, there are those who abuse the freedom it infers. A couple of times I've come across abandoned camps with rubbish strewn about, tents still standing and the odd sleeping bag hanging from a nearby branch. The cheapness of basic camping equipment mean that for some lazy people it's easier to just leave everything behind after a single use than bother tidying up. Anyway, the land access laws are a good thing.

My bike for the ride was a Specialised Rockhopper, famous in the mountain bike world at the time for being both relatively cheap and relatively good. Unfortunately, the front coil suspension forks were extremely heavy and I didn't fancy hauling them about on a road trip. So I wombled a much lighter solid front fork off of another biking friend and stuck those on the bike instead. Although they fitted, I couldn't get the head cap to fit, and not realising at the time that it was more than cosmetic in that it tensions the whole fork/headset up. I simply did without it and relied on the clamping of the stem to hold everything together..... whoops.

Day 1

And so, with little in the way of organisation except for a few maps I'd printed off and a rough plan, I set off on the drive across from Edinburgh to Glasgow, where I picked Al up. We then continued onwards to Oban where we'd get the ferry across to Mull.

Oban is a small town variously know both as 'The gateway to the isles' and 'the seafood capital of Scotland'. The first, because it's the busiest terminal for Caledonian MacBrayne (or Cal Mac as most people refer to it), which is the main operator of passenger and vehicle ferries between the mainland and 22 or so of the islands off of the west coast.

During the Second World War the natural defences around Oban made it ideal for a backup harbour for the merchant ships crossing the Atlantic. Here they would gather before joining large convoys for safety on their onwards trips out on the open sea. Oban was one of a few harbours to have submarine loops installed under the sea as an experiment. These loops of cable were placed on the sea bed across the approach channels. They were able to detect the magnetic disturbance of steel hulled vessels passing over them. Lookouts on the shore would report when it was a known ship. Presumably when they couldn't see anything, that would indicate that the signal may be a submarine entering the harbour.

While I drove my ancient Volvo, which always came with some slight added anxiety as it was generally on the brink of breaking down, Al spent the journey choosing from, and making occasional dismissive comments about my music collection, while examining the maps for our trip. Arriving in Oban, we stopped at a supermarket to stock up on food and then we came to the first problem, where to park? The only car parks in town were all pay and display. There was some long term parking just around from the ferry terminal but it was still expensive. I explored some back roads until we found a quiet street on a hill to abandon the car in. We unloaded and used our bikes to make our way back to the centre of town.

We bought our tickets for the ferry and then waited in the heavy drizzle. The sky was the same grey as the sea. The small island of Kerrera, lying just off the coast of Oban, was invisible. Like fireflies in the dark, luminous waterproof jacketed tourists milled around the harbour. As I stood watching, and wondering what the weather had in store for us over the next few days, I realised that I'd forgotten to pack a bike lock. I didn't think we'd need anything serious on a quiet island, so I went into a nearby hardware shop and bought one for £1.99. It would stop someone walking off with our bikes, but not much else. However, it was also very light, just being a thin cable with a lock on the end, so would do the job.

A hot coffee later, and the ferry had arrived. Like a sick whale it opened its giant mouth and vomited it's cargo of people and cars onto the dockside. Soon, it was our turn to be devoured.

Cycling onto a ferry is a bit odd. They don't let you actually ride your bike onto the ferry along with the cars (later we found we could get away with this if we were quick). You aren't allowed along the passenger only walkway. You have to wait till they tell you and then push your bike down the (sometimes surprisingly long) ramp and on, sometimes followed by a slow line of cars crawling behind like a funeral procession. Then you need to find the area for bikes. Here there are some thick straps attached to the wall which are used to tie the bikes up so they can't fall about in rough weather. Finally you are free to drag your panniers up about 5 flights of stairs and find somewhere to leave them. Once we'd completed these tasks, we settled in for the short 45 minute trip across to Craignure.

By the time we arrived it was already the middle of the afternoon, we were keen to get cycling and so didn't stick around. We pushed our bikes off of the good ship 'MV Isle of Mull' and immediately headed south. Al was faster and fitter than me and he sped off ahead. A short time later I caught up with him standing at

75

a junction waiting. "Which way?" he asked. I replied "I don't know, we'll need to look at the maps". Then we both stood about for a minute or so, before he said "So........maps?"
I looked at him. "You were looking at the maps in the car, I don't have them!" I'd assumed he'd put the maps in his bag. Turns out, we'd left the only maps in the car.

We headed on, relying on our wits and the tiny map on the back of a crumpled leaflet to guide us.

Suddenly, it started raining. A downpour of the heaviest rain possible. The kind of big droplets where you feel each one as it hits. We changed from being completely dry, to being soaked through in about three seconds. Luckily it was a warm day so it wasn't too unpleasant. A little further along the road we were treated to an impressive rainbow. I took some photos of Al trying to pose with his bike in front of it while the rain continued. I'm not sure the results matched whatever his expectations had been. We may not have known exactly where we were, but it didn't matter.

The road once again reached down to the coast. Just as we were pedalling along looking out to sea, I heard a "bollocks!", and turned around to see Al slowing down and looking at his back wheel. "I think I've got a puncture", he pulled over to the side of the road. The rain had stopped and so, while he fettled and swore a few times at his tyre, I lay on a rock looking out to sea, making little effort to help, other than to pass comment on his tyre removal technique. It didn't take long to fix the puncture and soon enough, the wheel was reattached to the bike and Al was happily pumping away. It gave me time to eat some snacks and have a rest from the relentless pace he was setting. The sun came out and warmed me up. I watched the sea calmly lapping at the shore as the sun shone.

We trekked on along the quiet roads and began looking for a suitable camp spot as the light began to fade. As we passed over the top of a hill the ocean opened out before us and a huge cliff spread steeply and spectacularly out to the west. The sun was beginning to set and the sky turned dusky red. It was an awesome sight. We stopped for a while in total silence, taking it all in.

Soon enough we had to move. There wasn't anywhere here

we could see that was suitable to camp. We cycled on for several kilometres along the rapidly darkening road. As we rounded a corner, it was clear the road continued for some way along the base of some steep cliffs and what flattish areas there were, were covered in rocks. The only area which might be all right was small and squashed between the road and the sea below. We decided it wasn't ideal but it would have to do.

We climbed over the crash barrier at the road's edge and set up camp just metres away on the other side. The stove was dug out and we cooked by torchlight. Now the sun had gone it was freezing. Not unexpected for late September.

After eating, we were disturbed by a strange honking noise coming from the darkness. A little investigation with our torches revealed nothing. We sat down to enjoy some whisky. After a few minutes the honking returned. Again, we could see nothing. Then it stopped. It may have been sneak enemy sub attack, or more likely, it was just an inquisitive seal. Once tucked up in my cosy sleeping bag I fell asleep easily. I was worn out. Any worries about traffic on the road disturbing us were unfounded. Nothing passed in the night.

The wind decided to get up in the early hours. I awoke to find the tent bent over, pressing into my face. I'd set the tent up so that I'd open the door to the sea in the morning. But my old, reliable tent which was generally fine had a flaw when the wind came from a certain direction. I turned around to point my feet into the collapsing end of the tent and went back to sleep, confident that the bendy fibreglass tent poles would hold out and spring back into shape as soon as the wind eased.

Day 2

The next morning I woke late at 10, and opened the tent door to a fantastic view. Just across from us was the island of Inch Kenneth.

Once owned by the Mitford family, it was where the famous Nazi sympathizer, Unity Mitford spent her last years before her death in 1948. She was born in London, the fifth of seven children, and was apparently somewhat aptly conceived in the town of Swastika, Ontario. In a biography it's speculated that being the younger sister of several clever, beautiful sisters meant that the only way Unity could get attention was to shock.

It's fair to say that Unity became obsessed with the Nazis, she learnt fluent German and greeted everyone with the Nazi salute "Heil Hitler".

Later she travelled to Munich with the aim of meeting Hitler. She not only succeeded, but joined the Nazi elite circle.

However, when the war started, she was confused as to her loyalties and during a difficult period shot herself in the head. She survived, but was never the same, and was looked after on the island until her death. She was welcomed into the local community, even though they disagreed with her politics, and was often see at local dances on Mull.

The island was an inheritance from their mother and one of the sisters, Jessica, a staunch communist, teased her sisters that she wanted the island to become a Soviet submarine base. It is now owned by Charles Darwin's great grand-daughter.

After a sleepy breakfast we consulted our 'map' and headed off again. The road followed the coast, with the cliffs looming over us, until we reached the end of the sea loch and then started back up the other side. Soon enough we were heading along the sea proper again, and up a 15% incline. My 3kg tent was holding me back as Al disappeared into the distance once again. I caught up at the spectacular Eas Fors waterfall falling 100ft straight into the sea below. We climbed down from the road to take a better look.

Eas Fors waterfall is tautological. Eas is Galic for waterfall and Fors, Viking Norse for waterfall. This often happens when the descriptor from one language is used as a name along with the descriptor of the second language. But it certainly made it easy for travellers and locals alike.

After exploring the paths around the top of the waterfall and having some refreshments we set off once again. Riding along the edge of a cliff meant that we had a great view out to sea and across the island of Ulva. I was still keeping an eye out for whales.

We took a left down to the waterfront and the dock for the ferry across to the island. We were thinking about making the trip across, but in the end decided not to. Maybe if we'd had a proper map and seen just how empty the island is we may have changed our minds. Cycling is welcomed on the rough tracks of the island and we could have wild camped on one of the remote beaches. It's also supposed to be fantastic for wildlife spotting.

We also could have visited Cairistiona's rock. She was the eldest daughter in a family of kelp harvesters and after a hunk of cheese went missing from the larder she accused her younger sister of the theft. Unaware of modern conventions regarding torture, she lowered the sister off a cliff with a thick cloth around her neck hoping for a confession. The cloth slipped and the sister fell to her death. Horrified, she ran back and told her parents about it. The village elders were notified and condemned Cairistiona to death. This was not to be any kind of quick process. She was sewn into a sack and placed on a rock at low tide. The villagers waited and watched as she slowly drowned with the incoming tide. Lovely.

I once lowered my brother off a small cliff with a rope slip-knotted around his waist. Luckily he survived, although he was a bit angry when, after complaining that the rope was tightening and he could no longer breathe, I released him into the river below.

Still on the main, bigger, island, we carried on up the tiny single track road, still following the coast. Just before we reached the small settlement of Calgary, there was a sheltered sandy beach. Amazing though it looked, we didn't stop as it was busy with tents and camper vans. In Calgary itself we came across an arts centre which also had a coffee shop. No discussion was necessary, we went in. I ordered a coke, a coffee and a huge piece of millionaire's shortbread. Clearly my body was craving sugar......and my brain was in no position to argue.

We continued on to Dervaig (Viking Norse for 'good inlet') at the head of Loch a'Chumhainn. The sun was out again and highlighted the strange white circular church spire as we approached the village. Apparently the local joke is that the church was designed by NASA.

There is a supposedly controversial stained glass window in the church from 1904 which alludes to Mary Magdelene (the one who travelled with Jesus as a follower, was a prostitute and was supposedly also present at the crucifixion and resurrection) being pregnant with the child of Jesus. An idea which has recently gained traction, mainly from the fictional book; 'The daVinci code'. Many tourists come here after reading the book just to see it.

Anyway, not being religiously inclined, we didn't bother with the church, we went to the pub instead. We ordered and drank a couple of very enjoyable pints outside in the beer garden. We spread out a giant map of Scotland we'd borrowed from the bar on the table and peered at the very small scale island. It was clear we were running out of Mull. We had a couple of days left, but it looked like we'd complete the whole circuit of the island today if we continued around the main road. We decided to make a detour to the remote Ardnamurchan peninsula on the mainland. It was a short ferry hop across from Tobermory.

Leaving the pub behind, we struggled over the hill behind Dervaig. The beer wasn't helping much. I dare say I was maybe even regretting the beer.

As we came down a small hill, we passed the end of a valley

containing Loch Frisa. The only road leading along the bottom of the valley was a dirt track. It was down here that is apparently the best place to see white-tailed eagles. We were tempted, but decided, for the moment, to stick to our plan and head on to Tobermory.

After the arduous climb, some signposts indicated that we were now passing the farm that is the home of Isle of Mull cheese. Then came the downhill. All the way into town. It was fun. I hit a bump and one of my panniers fell off and slid into the middle of the road. By the time I stopped I was way down the hill and had to climb back up while hoping that nothing else came down the road to crush my possessions. Luckily, nothing did. I clipped the pannier back on, making sure to attach the security strap this time and caught up with Al who was waiting at the sea front.

A quick shop to buy food and fuel for the stove, and we were ready to go. Tickets for the ferry bought, we had a bit of time to waste. So we went for a quick look about in Tobermory. Famous for its brightly coloured houses along the sea-front, Tobermory was built as a fishing port in the late 18th century, and is now the main town on Mull.

Supposedly, there is a wrecked Spanish galleon at the bottom of the bay. The story goes that after Sir Francis Drake's success over the Spanish armada, some of the ships escaped north. One of them stopped and filled up with supplies at Tobermory and then tried to leave without paying for them. Donald Maclean of Duart reportedly managed to board the ship and set fire to it. When the fire reached the gunpowder magazine, it exploded and sank, along with 100 crew and its millions of gold coins. However, the exact location isn't known and no-one has ever found any trace of the ship.....if in fact it's anything more than a story.

Many people have tried to find the treasure, most recently an aristocrat; Sir Torquhil Ian Campbell who is the 13th Duke of Argyll. Along with some investors, he has commissioned several dive expeditions. Apparently his family were given the sole rights to the ship's contents. Who gave them the rights? Doesn't the Queen own everything hauled up from the depths? I suspect the Queen is trolling the Duke after he accidentally stepped on a corgi or something. She knows there's nothing down there.

We boarded the ferry and this being a small boat, we didn't have to endure the funeral procession. The sun which had been shining up until now disappeared behind some thick grey clouds. Sitting up on the open deck, it was freezing. But still hopeful of catching a glimpse of a whale I endured it for a while. We slid away from the small dock and slowly made our way out past sailing boats and dinghys moored in the bay. Once out on the sea, I watched as Mull grew smaller and blacker, the dark mounds of the island merging with those of the distant mainland to the south.

The end of Ardnamurchan peninsula, towards which we were heading, is basically a huge crater made up of several concentric rings. This was created by a volcano some 58 million years ago, about the time when Greenland broke off and started moving away. This makes for an interesting landscape.

A Viking ship was recently found on Ardnamurchan, the first complete ship burial found in Britain. Unfortunately not much was left of the timbers, but the outline of the boat and many rivets could clearly be seen in the soil. Amongst the burial possessions were found a highly decorated sword, a Norwegian whetstone, a bronze ring-pin from Ireland, a spear and a shield. Whoever it was must have been quite a high ranking individual. Sometimes their loved ones were buried alive alongside.

In the 10th Century, an Arab writer named Ahmad ibn Fadlan produced a description of a Viking funeral he witnessed. The dead Chieftain was buried in a temporary grave while they prepared. They made some burial clothes and a woman who volunteered to join him in the afterlife was drugged before having sex with each of the remaining men. An old woman, known as 'The angel of death', was responsible for organising the ritual. The volunteer, now in drugged trance, was lifted over a door frame so that she could see into the realm of the dead. Her jewellery was taken and shared out between the angel of death and the other girls.

As she was fed more liquid drugs, she was raped and then stabbed between the ribs by the 'angel'. The boat was finally set alight (on land) with the dead Chieftain and the volunteer aboard. Afterwards, it was buried with rocks.

The mainland was reached without any sightings of sea life and we left the ferry via the desolate terminal.

Passing through the tiny hamlet of Kilchoan, my legs were beginning to get extremely weary from cycling so hard to keep up with Al. For a while I found myself fantasising about stopping, climbing off off of my bike and lying down. I lost all motivation to try and keep up, and dropped back, slowing to a more comfortable pace.

We climbed up the edge of the crater (it sounds spectacular, but from the ground it just looks like another hill) and down the other side into the centre before crossing over crater floor.

I could never have guessed if I hadn't know, that we were now in the heart of the giant crater. The landscape was a bit strange, subtly different from that which had come before. The vast area between the outer ring of hills was for the most part flat with either short and rough grass growing, like in public park, or longer clumps of grass browning in the sun. There was a definite reduction in heather. The centre of the crater was higher than the rest with the concentric circles of the hills rippling outward like a frozen moment in time just after dropping a pebble into a flat puddle.

There isn't anything but the road, and a single farm, 'Achnaha', sitting in the greenest patch of the crater. Then it was time to go up and over the other side.

Below us now was Sanna Bay, with its sparse collection of houses. It was getting late and the light was disappearing so we decided to speed down the hill, hoping to find somewhere to camp on the coast or beach. Unfortunately, the houses were quite close to anywhere that looked reasonable. And the main beach looked tricky to get to with our bikes. With no other options we started back up the road looking for the first decent place to camp. On the way back up the hill, with exhaustion taking hold, I could see a possible spot a bit of a walk off to the side. I think Al was wanting to continue on and find a more accessible place next to the road. But I persuaded him and we set off and found a great spot, in the back of my mind was the view we'd wake up to from here in the morning.

On unpacking Al pulled pulled out a silk liner for his sleeping bag and spun it around to air it. I hadn't seen it till now. Nice to bring a bit of luxury when everything else is slightly damp and sweaty.

I once went on a camping trip with Al and another friend in the beautiful Glen Affric, just north of Loch Ness. After sharing out the load of food and splitting the tents and equipment between the three of us, we set off. Al was constantly up ahead, even though we weren't exactly taking it easy at the back. Another friend had trouble crossing a tiny stream due to the weight of his backpack. Somehow he tried to jump across, didn't make it, and spun around in a ridiculous way on landing before falling backwards onto the bank, his feet still in the water. Luckily for him I caught this all on camera. Anyway, when we arrived at a suitable spot for camping, we set up the tents, then to our surprise Al pulled a plump, full size pillow from his backpack!

Back on Ardnamurchan, once the tents were up, we set up the stove on a flat rocky outcrop not far away, and drank whisky while our dinner of tomatoes, beans and pasta cooked. We weren't drinking to get particularly drunk, that's not really the point, savouring the whisky itself is the point and the conversation that goes with it. Life doesn't get much better than this.

I climbed into bed, and slept very well.......even though I didn't have a silk sleeping bag liner.

Day 3

I woke up in the searing heat building up in the tent from the sun and pulled the zip on the door up to let some fresh air in. The view was pretty amazing. The white sandy beach stretched along the coast below, beyond the turquoise sea was utterly flat and calm. And further up the coast, clouds were streaming off the top of the mountains of Skye, the Cuillins. We ate breakfast, taking in the view wordlessly.

Taking a look at our leaflet/map, we decided to make a detour out to the Ardnamurchan lighthouse, also the most westerly point of the British mainland.

After cycling back through the crater, we took a right up the tiny road which led to the lighthouse. The road was flooded and without really stopping to check how deep it was, we ploughed on through feet in the air, trying not to get soaked.

Arriving at the lighthouse, I was surprised and happy to find a nice café. We dumped the bikes and walked the path up to the base of the lighthouse.

It's a pretty impressive structure and although it was designed by the Stevenson family (like nearly all the lighthouses in Scotland), this one had a different Egyptian style (No I don't really know what that means either, given that it looked like a normal tube shaped lighthouse, but it said it in the visitor centre so it must be true). I hadn't really thought about it before, but I learnt that great carved stones making up the walls aren't joined with any kind of mortar. The blocks are carved in such a way that they slot strongly together while allowing for some movement. In a strong storm the top of the otherwise solid looking lighthouse actually sways.

This tower first shone out and warned sailors of the location of the rocky coast in October 1849. Two years later it was damaged by lightning strikes during a particularly bad storm and it's hard to imagine, given the difference in height between the base and the sea far below, but some huge waves also washed some of the lower walls and access road away.

Personally, I liked the mighty foghorn painted bright red which emerged from the ground like something from a surreal cartoon and pointed out to sea from the rocks in front of the lighthouse. Judging by the size of the thing, I imagine it would be very loud. Unfortunately, I'd wouldn't be hearing it as it's no longer operational.

I'd read that the point on which the lighthouse sat was a great area for spotting whales, I stared out to sea for a while focusing on any dark spots or inconsistencies on the surface, but I didn't spot anything of interest. Maybe the sea was too choppy. Perhaps whales will be like red squirrels for me; I hadn't seen a red squirrel despite keeping an eye out for years. One day I stopped off at a forested hill in Braemar especially to see them and during a long walk spotted a couple. Since that day, they appear to me everywhere. I've probably seen a hundred. The best sighting was of one stealing food from a bird feeder attached to a living room window while I stood watching, unnoticed, a few feet away. I'm hoping than once I finally spot a whale, a similar sort of Baader-Meinhof phenomenon will also occur. A few months after that and I'll lose interest and move onto spotting some other elusive creature.

We went to the café. I'm not sure why, but the further west in Scotland you go the better the coffee and cakes seem to be. I'm not particularly fickle about my coffee, but I know the difference between proper fresh coffee rather than instant or something that's been sitting a pot. I used to think I didn't like it at all when growing up, but I'd just never been given the chance to drink anything that wasn't freeze or spray-dried, and assumed that was what all coffee was supposed to be. It could be that the higher standards of remote areas are at least partly due of the limited customer base meaning they can't afford to put customers off. Or maybe they are just intent on delivering a quality service rather than just milking people for all they can.

It was time to head off again. We were aiming to make it back to the ferry in time for the return trip to Mull. Looking at my watch I realised we'd spent too long enjoying the café and we were late, late, late. The ferry after the next one wasn't until the evening. Not wanting to spend the rest of the day here, we pedalled on, luckily it was mostly easy riding or downhill. With the ferry pier in sight, we could see that the ferry was docked. Pushing on, I felt slightly anxious, thinking that it's probably going to leave just a moment before we arrive. We raced along the last section of road turning down the small side road that took us to the boat. We hopped aboard. We'd made it! Then we waited for twenty minutes for no apparent reason before it finally groaned into life, poured a cloud of dark smoke into the sky, and slowly set off across the water to the island again.

Just as on the ferry trip out, I froze up on deck while keeping a lookout once again in case an elusive whale should decide to pop its head up, although the sea was more choppy this time so the chances were slim anyway.

Back on the island, we retraced our bike wheel tracks out of Tobermory up the steep hill. We still had another night left, but if we headed back down the eastern side of the island, we'd be done in a couple of hours. Instead we rode back to the track road we'd seen heading south down the interior of the island. This track was where the white-tailed eagles of mull were supposed to hang out.

Pointing our wheels down the valley, I was at first happy to be off of the tarmac. The complete absence of cars was great. Usually a mountain biker rather than road rider, I was used to cycling off-road. However, for this trip we both had high pressure slick tyres on our bikes, not ideal for a bumpy rough gravel covered track. As I rolled along, my handlebars felt like they were vibrating over every individual molecule in the road. Al's tyres being even

87

thinner than mine, he soon fell behind even my current sedate pace. I turned and could see him weaving through the worst of the pot-holes. My old suspension forks would have been useful now to absorb the worst bumps.

The sun came out as our route took us along the side of a hill some way above the loch which stretched out before us to the south. We stopped to admire the view for a moment. There was not a single bird to be seen, never mind a huge, broad winged eagle.

For another hour and a half we slowly took our time along the valley until eventually we reached the main hide for watching the eagles. Nothing...the sky was still empty. We continued past.

Finally, leaving the slippery gravel of the track road behind, we headed back down to the coast and along to the village of Salen. The Salen hotel had a small outdoor beer garden which was too inviting to ignore.

The full name of the village is 'Sàilean Dubh Chaluim Chille' which translates as 'the black little bay of St Columba'. St Columba at one time regularly preached from the rocks right behind the Salen hotel, although apparently almost none of the villagers bothered to turn up to listen so he gave up and moved on. That fact alone made me like this village.

Looking at the map again, it was clear that it wasn't too far back down to Craignure where we'd eventually need to get the ferry back to Oban. We had a couple of pints in the sun and Al came up with a plan for our last night of camping. He wanted to go straight past the ferry terminal and re-cover our tracks to the south end of the island, except this time we'd go down the small track we'd previously ignored which headed right down to the coast and around a small peninsula where hopefully we'd find a nice quiet spot to camp. It looked interesting.

After lazing in the sun and watching people going about their business for far too long, we raced off down the coast road. Instead of a short trip back to the ferry, we now had a fairly long ride ahead of us. With two pints inside me, and the sun shining, I again gave up trying to keep up with Al and lost sight of him soon after we started.

This part of the coast was beautiful though. I passed some old wooden boats listing over on their sides on the sand next to a pier. A quick stop was required in order to take some photos.

Further on, I finally caught up with Al who was waiting by the road just before the ferry town of Craignure. By now my legs were aching again trying to keep up. I was regretting not taking clip-less pedals like he had. Clip-less is a rubbish name for them though, as you still clip your feet into them. They should have been called something like 'clip-in pedals' as they evolved from the old style 'toe-clip' pedals with straps to tighten around your shoes. Apparently, the counter-intuitive name originated in the Tour de France when people first saw Bernard Hinault and Greg Lemond (both tour winners) cycling without the metal foot cages and straps everyone else was using. In fact they were both making use of a new pedal design from 'Look', who, up until then had been a ski binding manufacturer. The lack of visible toe-clips led people to call them 'clip-less', although the shoes were instead now physically attached to pedal by small cleats on the underside of the shoe which attach to a connection on the pedal. The rider can disconnect from the pedal by twisting their heel out.

The pedals supposedly save up to 20% of your energy as well as allowing you to share the pedalling load between different muscles as you can not only push down on the pedals, but pull up as well. The fact that Al had the pedals and I didn't, was, I like to think, making all the difference.

We pushed on through Craignure, stopping only to buy some Snickers and a Coke on the way through. That Coke was good though! Sugary snacks never taste better than when you are completely knackered and your body is crying out for quick energy.

Anyway, I continued on and watched Al disappear ahead once again. I was beginning to really struggle now, but I also knew it couldn't be too much further. We took the turning onto the small road south and as Al seemingly effortlessly climbed the short but steep inclines, I slowly worked away, painfully turning the pedals.

The road seemed endless, although it was only about ten kilometres long. The weight of my panniers was killing me. My legs had now completely given up after only several days of adventure. How did Al get so much better at cycling than me? I blamed my working in an office with only a 15 minute commute, handy though that was.

We stopped by the sea and climbed a small grassy slope off the road to a nice spot overlooking the inlet of Loch Spelve before us.

We were on one the wildest and least visited parts of the island, the only hamlet of note being Lochbuie. From the Gaelic "Loch Buidhe" which means "yellow loch".

Samuel Johnson was a famous visitor here. He was most famous for compiling "A dictionary of the English Language" in 1755 entirely by himself. It was another 150 years before the Oxford English Dictionary was completed. Johnson's book has been ranked one of the greatest single achievements of scholarship by a single individual. Although it wasn't a defined illness at the time, his strange mannerisms and tics point to him having suffered from Tourette's syndrome.

One of his many quotes was "The use of travelling is to regulate imagination by reality, and instead of thinking how things may be, to see them as they are." It seemed apt for our current situation.

For the last time on this short trip, I surveyed the ground for a flat, comfortable tent sized area free from rocks and sheep poo. The poles were quickly fed through the blue, waterproof, material and the tent pegs were, with some difficulty, hammered into the earth with a small rock. Stoves were dug out and twisted onto gas canisters. After cooking up the last of our food and eating all the snacks I had left, we finished the last drops of whisky and the conversation flowed. Soon enough the last of the light disappeared and it was time to climb into my sleeping bag and stretch out my tired legs on my camping mat. I had another great night's sleep.

Day 4

I awoke. The sun was again heating up the confined space of my tent to an almost unbearable degree. I unzipped the door to find sheep blocking the view of the water below. They soon moved on and I lay for quite a while enjoying the quiet of the morning and watching the birds circling above the shore. Sleeping in a tent is a wonderful thing, the satisfaction of sleeping somewhere temporary, the thin, permeable walls allowing the smells and sounds of the surroundings to come to the front of your consciousness. Small animals snuffling around sound as loud as deer, deer sound like monsters in the night. Yet we can still feel completely secure and at ease zipped up in a warm sleeping bag.

Eventually, Al shouted out to ask if I was awake and we got up and ate breakfast.

We packed up for the last time and headed down the hill on our bikes. Al singing loudly as the sheep ran before him.

There was one final puncture for Al to fix while I had a nap in the heather at the side of the road overlooking an inlet, before we made our way back to Craignure and the Ferry.

For once we'd timed it near perfectly. There was no rushing today. Neither was there any hanging around. We pushed down the ramps, tied our bikes up once more and headed to the top deck where we watched as Mull grew more distant.

I kept a lookout from a windy viewpoint....still no whales.

Ben Alder Route:

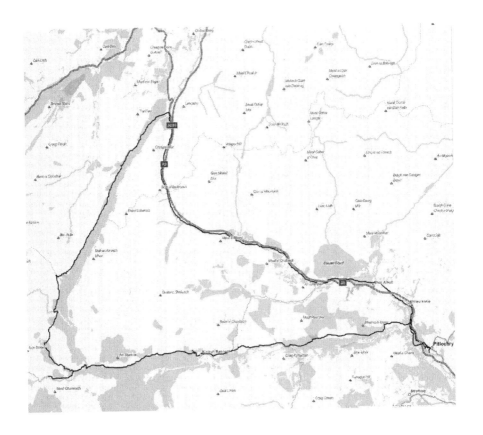

Ben Alder

It was the middle of winter. One of the wettest, most miserable winters in living memory. The news was filled with reports of floods in Yorkshire, Perthshire and the north-east of Scotland. People were fleeing their homes as the water levels rose. Reporters stood in the water as deep as they dare as they were filmed talking while household items such as fridges dramatically floated past. The met office and SEPA were pumping out reports about the rainfall being the heaviest since records began. The army was pumping out pensioners living rooms.

It was while all this was going on that Jay and I decided to make a mini bike trip up to Ben Alder bothy over a couple of days. We didn't really have much of a plan before the trip. Due to other commitments it was quite a while before we finally settled on a weekend. I was concerned about the weather, it hadn't stopped raining all that week. The Friday beforehand, I was at work, and looked at the weather forecast several times during the day. It looked pretty bad. Snow was forecast, the weekend was going to be the coldest for some time. Where there wasn't snow there were weather warnings about torrential rain and flooding. I got home and switched the TV on to see a weather report showing a map covered in snow and red wind warnings. It didn't look pleasant.

Still, we live in Scotland. The weather is regularly awful. I phoned Jay. He was also slightly worried, but we decided to go anyway. The forecast is often wrong. Generally, I ignore it when planning outdoors activities. If it's pouring when I wake up, then I might change plans, but otherwise if I planned things by the forecast, I'd rarely do anything. Often, it not nearly as bad as it's supposed to be. Often, it actually nice out when the forecast said it was going to be apocalyptic. We spoke about the route. It had a long road section at the start with a small village and hotel at an appropriate point for having a hot dinner. If the weather was indeed terrible, then we could easily abort up until this point and ride back to the start.

So we decided to go for it. I packed everything. Then, later while I was sitting back watching tv, enjoying a glass of wine, a niggling concern about getting soaked in the middle of nowhere entered my head, prompting me to return to my pile of cycling stuff, unpack some non-essentials such as my comfy blow-up pillow and add more clothes instead. I needed to be able to be able to change into something dry if we did get badly caught out. As we were planning to eat at the hotel in the evening, I just packed some snack bars, a bag of cereal for breakfast (with milk power) and a single super-noodle pack (as it weighs practically nothing) for emergencies as well as lots of tea bags.

Jay had some things to do the next morning, so it was a late start. I arrived at his house at lunch time, and after transferring my stuff to his camper van we finally set off for the hour and a half drive to our start point in the town of Pitlochry.

The rain didn't let up for almost the whole drive. We stopped off at a supermarket for Jay to stock up on food. They were busy pumping water out of the car park and drying the shop by switching the air conditioning to the maximum. It was freezing in there. The manager was walking around in a t-shirt as if to prove to his staff that it really wasn't that cold. He wasn't fooling anyone though. While I waited and shivered, I bought a pork pie and some sandwiches to have for lunch on the second day and looked at the papers. The headlines were all about the weather which at least was relevant to our current situation. I always remember reading that on the day after the outbreak of World War One, the main Aberdeenshire paper (which is still going) had the headline "Giant neep found in Turriff" ('neep' being the Scottish word for turnip). It also apparently brilliantly reported "Local man in boating accident" regarding the sinking of the Titanic.

We parked up in the driveway of a house owned by an absent friend of Jays and quickly got changed and strapped various things onto our bikes. Miraculously, while we were busy, it stopped raining!

"Ready to go?" asked Jay, "Not really", I replied shivering in my cycling clothes. I had decided to dress fairly lightly for the moment as I tend to warm up quickly while cycling. I didn't want to have to stop in ten minutes in order to strip off some layers. We headed off down the hill, crossed the swollen river via a Victorian suspension footbridge (which I shamefully remember drunkenly having peed off of a long time ago when I lived and worked here for a few months during a long, hot, summer break from university). Making our way through town, we quickly left the tarmac behind and instead worked our way along the, much more interesting and fun, rooty footpaths running along the edge of loch Faskally. The cold air from the loch had kept the mud frozen making it an easy, if bumpy ride. A few quick kilometres later, we were approaching a footbridge back across the river which we needed to make use of. Some ominous signs warned it was closed. As we arrived we could see it was properly closed. A storm the week before and the incessant rain had apparently damaged the foundations of the bridge meaning that it was in imminent danger of collapsing into the deep gorge below. Not wanting to join the bridge it if it did collapse, we followed the instruction not to cross. Instead we carried our laden bikes up a steep embankment, then up some steep steps, then up and over pedestrian bridge crossing a railway line, then up the steep incline the far side until we finally reached a road. Heavily loaded bikes aren't easy to lift. Barely 30 minutes after starting out, we were already suffering.

Cycling back towards Pitlochry again for a short distance, we took the first turn-off and then finally made it to the other side of the river via the road bridge. It was getting properly dark by now. I could still see well enough, but dug my lights out of my backpack anyway for safety. The next section was on road, albeit a very quiet road.

I switched my head-torch on to light a small patch of the road in front. Jay switched on his head-torch.....which completely obliterated my pathetic beam of light. "Hmm.....I might need to upgrade" I thought to myself. The rain started up as we hit the first of the hills.

Working our way along the road, it quickly became apparent we were going to have to rely on GPS to see how far along the road we were, it really was pitch dark. I cycled alongside Jay, taking advantage of his more powerful lights to see where we were going. Several times, usually when cars passed and we had to go in single file, he disappeared off into the distance while I struggled on with my dimming head torch. I'd charged up some batteries the night before, but either they were being affected by the cold, or they were losing their ability to hold charge. Switching in some spares did little better. Next time I'm just going buy some proper fresh batteries.

One time he got even further ahead and I struggled to catch up as I watched his light disappearing down and to the left over a bridge ahead. He waited and then shouted back "hey, you look like someone coming along the road with a candle back there!"

We chatted as we rode the next thirty kilometres along the road. Rain turned to snow for a period and then back to rain. At one point while climbing a hill Jay commented "Whoa...I'm suddenly really hot! "Weirdly, so am I" I replied "it feels like the air is suddenly getting much warmer. This is really strange".

We reached the village of Tummel Bridge and rolled along the main street looking for a place to eat. It was very quiet. A well-wrapped up couple were walking along the street carrying a bottle of wine. Skidding to a stop on the icy road in front of them, we asked if there was anywhere open nearby. The man looked at us like we were crazy and then shook his head slowly. "The hotel here is closed for winter, there's nothing else open" the woman said. "What about further along at Kinnloch Rannoch?" Jay asked about the next village about ten kilometres along the road. "I think MacDonalds will be open" came the reply. We realised they were referring to the hotel and resort chain rather than the American burger shop, but we joked about it with them anyway before saying our thanks and cycling off.

As we carried on it began to gently snow again. This was much preferable to rain though as snow tends to just fall off of jacket fabric rather than soaking in. We had some great conversation

96

as we cycled along. It took our minds off the cold for a while and stopped us from questioning what the hell we were doing out here, when we could have been back home, comfortable and warm.

After some time we rode into Kinloch Rannoch with one thought on our minds; hot food. I wondered what would be on the menu. I hoped for a hot steak pie, or some other equally hearty food, and maybe a nice beer to go with it. I hoped it wouldn't be a place of small portions and fancy food presentation. I needed food, and lots of it.

We quickly passed through the village to the far end where we knew the MacDonalds hotel was. Cycling up the short steep drive, I was excited at the prospect of stopping for a while. The lights of the hotel came into view and we passed a bar in a side extension. It was clearly closed, with shutters down over the bar and chairs up-ended on the tables. Why do they do this? Surely the last thing you want on the tables which people eat at is the area of the chair which is in contact with the bums of strangers. Come to think of it I wouldn't want the bums of people I know either.

We rode along the long hotel front until we reached the main door, beyond which we could see another tabled area, possibly the restaurant. It was in near darkness, illuminated by dim emergency lighting. "Oh shit! What's going on here?" I rode right up to the door. I could see a notice posted in the glass. "Closed for maintenance for three weeks" alongside the actual dates of closure. There was nothing to do but laugh. This trip wasn't going to plan. We weren't even off of the road section yet. I was freezing, and hungry. It started to rain heavily. Jay looked on in dismay. "Let's stop in here", I said heading into a covered car port at the side of the hotel. "Yeah, let's brew up" replied Jay, trying unconvincingly to sound upbeat.

We had just started unpacking a stove when I asked "you sure there's no other hotels here?"
"Yeah, think so. There's another one but I didn't notice it on the way through, it must be shut"
"Is it worth checking out? I don't mind going back for a quick look."
"hmmm...ok, but I'm pretty sure".

So, we remounted and rode back into the village. It quickly became apparent the hotel was shut. In fact it had been gutted. We could see some serious work was being carried out on its interior. We cycled off of the main road and over a bridge to check the other side of the river. There was nothing. We decided to head back to the car port and decide what to do.

On the way out of the village a brightly lit sign saying "Highland Club" caught our attentions. "What's a highland club?" I asked. "Dono..." Jay replied, riding off down the driveway beyond the sign. I followed him down to a car park at the far end. There was a brightly lit office with someone sitting inside. "Looks like a static caravan park" I thought to myself. Jay had parked up his bike and gone in the door. He was now speaking to a woman. I spiralled my bike around in the empty car park, keeping warm. After a few minutes Jay appeared at the door and with a grin shouted "you want tea or coffee?"

Opening the door, I was met with a blast of warm air. It was good to take my damp gloves off. "Hello!", the lady headed off down a corridor to the far end where she got busy with a kettle and some cups. "Thanks for inviting us in. What exactly is a Highland club?" I looked at some photos on the wall of some people dancing and dressed in tartan while others wore plastic horned Viking helmets. They looked like they were having a good time. I imagined we were in the headquarters of a social club of some sort. "We manage time-share apartments" the woman told us, "Here's your tea, and a wee cake to keep you going". Sure, it was no hotel and hot meal, but it was a vast improvement on being out it the freezing night. We chatted to the woman for half an hour or so. She told us about her collection of cats and dogs she homed when no-one else wanted them. We told her of our trip and where we were heading. She didn't seem at all concerned that we were about to head off the road and up into the mountains in the darkness on a snowy evening. It made me feel a bit less concerned. "Be careful, the roads are awfy icy at the moment", "do you need some batteries" she said opening a drawer after she noticed me fiddling with my head torch. "Thanks, but I've got spares. Think it's just the cold that's killing them". She then veered perilously close to racism and started telling us about the young people who come from all over to work at the resort. She was a bit derogatory towards the workers, then "I don't mind them foreigners as long as they do their job". It was all becoming slightly uncomfortable. We said goodbye and thanks, and left. I wasn't sure if she was just talking and it came out a bit wrong, rather than having any malice, Jay wasn't so sure.

Nice though the warm break and piece of cake had been, we still needed to eat. We headed back to the car port at the hotel where we quickly ate the sandwiches bought at the supermarket earlier. I opened a pack of M&Ms and we had a handful each. Hardly a proper meal for two hungry cyclists. While eating our 'meal' the topic of whether we should head back, aborting the trip, came up. But just for a moment. Neither of us were seriously thinking of giving up yet.

There was nothing to keep us in village for any longer. Heading off along the hotel driveway, we expected to re-join the main road at the far side. We quickly climbed a steep hill through some holiday apartments to find the drive ended with a locked gate blocking our way. "Dammit! We need to go back". Nothing major was really going wrong, but all these small issues were beginning to get tiresome.

Back on the road, we cycled along the road for a fairly pleasant sixteen kilometres further, now we were cycling along the edge of Loch Rannoch. Again the conversation was good and cheered me up. In fact we were so engrossed in our chat that we rode right past the turning we were supposed to take. Jay was keeping track of roughly where we were though, and realised we must be close to where we'd leave the road. He stopped to check the map, he thought it was little further on. In fact it was back one kilometre. I wondered to myself how far I would have kept going before thinking about where the turning was?

We found the track, double checked that it looked correct on the GPS, and then headed up to a large metal gate. We squeezed our laden bikes through the pedestrian side gate. On the other side I decided it was finally time to get my proper night biking light out.

It was bright enough, however, it had been very cheap when I bought it and was also now a few years old, so I didn't have too much faith that the accompanying power pack would last more than a couple of hours. I'd have to use it sparingly. Still, now we were on a rough track, the pathetically weak beam of my head torch would no longer suffice. I attached the proper light to my handlebars and switched it on.

Heading up the hill, I was riding slightly ahead of Jay. I turned a corner to see a stream of deer crossing the track up ahead. One after another they darted into the middle of the road, paused to look at the light, and then dived for cover in the thick trees.
"Did you see all the deer?" I asked when Jay caught up.
"Nope......deer? Where? How many?"
"Loads."

Upwards, we climbed through the forest, the road getting steadily more rocky as we went. As it got colder, it got easier. The mud hardened, and the rain stopped. It was a pretty good feeling to finally be off road. I stopped and pulled an extra t-shirt from my bag to put on. Soon we emerged from the forest. I say emerged, but in the claustrophobic darkness we could have been surrounded by anything and we wouldn't have known. I turned my light to point off into the darkness and saw nothing but heather. As we cycled on, strange and eerie glowing shapes would appear far off ahead or slightly off to the side. Mostly it was noticeable through my peripheral vision. Looking directly at the spots where the light appeared to be coming from I couldn't see anything. As the mysterious shapes floated through my vision, it was easy to see how people in the past came up with, and believed in, stories of apparitions and beings roaming the moorland at night. The stories of the ghost of Ben Alder cottage came to mind. As we got closer I realised they weren't spooky, ethereal phantasms, just rocks containing quartz, reflecting light.

It felt like we were now high up. Somewhere with a view. But I couldn't see anything. Not even any glow in the distance from the faraway lights of houses and cars. It was eerily dark. Imaginations can run wild thinking about the source of odd sights and sounds when your senses are heightened. Up here, tonight, there was no wind. It was completely still. Adding to the other worldliness of the situation.

A large rock clicked as my front tyre hit it and propelled it into my naked shin, "Oooowww!". I could see Jay's light further ahead swinging from side to side across the track as he manoeuvred his bike over bumps and around obstacles.

I'm not used to cycling in the dark, I don't do it often enough unless you count my commute to and from work in winter. I should do it more. It feels different to normal mountain biking. Familiar trails feel fresh and new. It becomes harder to keep track of where you are, how far you have to go. The terrain and obstacles appear without warning, there's less time to relax. Having no vistas to look at or views off to the sides focuses your attention on the small area directly in front. It's just an altogether different experience.....in a good way.

We raced down the hill at the far side, Jay disappeared off ahead. I don't know how he does it. He doesn't even have front suspension but somehow always gets away on the downhill sections. Maybe I'm getting too careful. A bit more climbing and then another descent through a forested area. We stopped for a rest and some more M&Ms. The trees were a frozen whitish shade of green, crystals of ice clinging to the pine needles. The steam from our breath drifted across and made cloudy patterns in our beams of light.

Continuing onwards we rolled down a hill and then the track swung to left. I thought we should now be very close to the edge of Loch Ericht. I couldn't see it though. I imagined the view in the daytime would be great. We were right at the south end of the water. Looking north the loch stretches for twenty-four kilometres with mountains along both edges. As it was, I couldn't see a thing. A further hundred metres along the track and we heard the lapping of water. Shining lights towards the sound showed our first sight of the choppy water. White foam was accumulating on the shore line.

Crossing a bridge, I turned my lights on the river below to see a jagged mess of ice on the surface. The water level must have recently dropped, pushing all the ice together like tectonic plates forming frozen mountains.

The road continued for a few more kilometres along the loch edge getting rougher the further we went. Finally it petered out and the only way forwards was along a rough path. Checking the GPS made it relatively easy to stick to the right path despite lots of turn-offs. The further we went, the boggier the ground was getting. More and more often I'd have to dismount to drag my bike out of the mud, or lift it over particularly un-cycleable sections. It was hard work, and I was hungry.

A couple of kilometres further, and the path disappeared as we followed it away from the loch. The ground was now impossible to cycle on. It was difficult enough to walk on. We jumped over icy ditches and puddles between the highest divots of heather and peat. Mostly the process was to push or lift my bike forwards a few feet, then use it to help keep my balance as I jumped to the next bit of dry looking ground, before repeating. It was extremely slow going. I spent a lot of time slipping over, jarring the knee I'd broken a while back. Jay, up ahead, seemed to be faring slightly better. His shoes, with clips for attaching to his bike pedals, had a recessed cleat meaning they were much better suited to walking in then my normal SPD type clip-in shoes. Then again, maybe he just had a better sense of balance. As we crossed the bog in what I would have sworn was a straight line, I noticed our track was veering to the left on the GPS. I knew we should trust the GPS, but the thought did cross my mind that it may have gone haywire. We tried to correct by heading back to the right A few minutes later I rechecked and we were heading left again. We were going much further up the hill than we should have been. I watched a documentary once where they tested people wearing blindfold to see if they could walk in a straight line. It was impossible, everyone veered off the route although when asked they were sure they were still going straight. I think we were suffering from the same effect, not having any discernible landmarks with which to tell where we were going. I made a considerable effort to keep turning slightly right hoping that that would either mean we were going straight, or take us back down to where we should have been. It didn't really work. The GPS was just showing a wiggly trail where we been.

Although fatigue was setting in, I knew we were getting close to the end of the day. The bothy wasn't far away now. I was in pretty good shape considering I'd been worried about getting a soaking by the rain, which in freezing temperatures could have been seriously bad. I was just thinking about this, when I came to a particularly wide ditch. I could have found a way around, but the ice I'd stood on so far seemed pretty thick. I was tired and getting complacent. I decided to chance it and stood in the middle of the ice. It held. I rolled my bike across beside me and then lifted it to get it over the hillock at the far side. Crack...I broke through the ice up to my ankles. "It's ok, it's not deep!" I laughed and shouted across to Jay who had turned to watch. Just as I said this, like a comedy, another crack sounded out, and I fell much deeper. Up to my waist and I was sinking fast. Quickly leaning forwards and putting my weight on my bike I was able to pull myself quickly out "Shiiiit!" When I stood up though, I was still remarkably dry. I think the mud was so cold it had frozen beneath the surface ice, and although I'd sunk into it, it wasn't wet enough to penetrate my shoes and waterproofs. I'd been lucky.

We continued onwards over the bog for what seemed like ages, but was probably only half an hour. Eventually, I could hear a river up ahead. A couple of minutes later and we arrived on its banks. "I think we're going to have to cross" Jay said. It looked possible to cross, but we'd probably get a good soaking at the very least. I didn't fancy it. "Hmm...let's take a look at the map first, figure out where we are" I retrieved my OS map from my backpack. "I think we're somewhere here" I pointed to a bend on a river on the map. "If it's this river then there's a bridge downstream somewhere". We followed the edge of the river. It was easier to walk here, I could actually push my bike most of the time. Soon enough, out of the darkness, a bridge appeared. A slightly dodgy looking bridge, but I'd take my chances. Hanging down by the side of the bridge were some snapped steel cables which at one time stretched to fixed points on the banks helping to keep the bridge stable. Another notable issue was that the area around the end of the bridge had been washed out by water, with the result that the bridge walkway started at about chest height. Jay went first, lifting his bike up and pushing it along a bit to give himself room to climb up behind. It looked pretty dodgy. I followed on behind shoving my bike up first as best I could while climbing up. Once on the bridge the space between the handrails was quite thin, but the bridge otherwise felt fine. Not as rickety or wobbly as it looked. I tentatively squeezed across with the water rushing past below and then dropped down again at the other side. Excellent, we really were getting close now.

The map showed the bothy as being just along a little from the bridge. Pointing our bike lights into the darkness showed nothing. We walked on through a flatter but particularly boggy section alongside a fence. And then in front of us something glinted. We walked closer, and.......finally.......the building came into sight. I was not only relieved to finally have reached our home for the night, but I was relieved to see it was in darkness, meaning that probably no-one else was there. I wasn't sure I'd have had the energy left to make much conversation with strangers.

Trying the front door, it wouldn't open. A bit of further investigation and both of us giving a good push and it finally burst open. I think the latch was just stuck or frozen. For a small moment I did wonder if we were going to get in. Exploring the bothy I went into the middle room, which was small and empty but for a couple of hard wooden beds recessed into the wall. Jay went into the room on the left. I heard "Ohh sorry buddy! Hope I didn't wake you? Thought we were alone in here. We'll go through to the other room", evidently someone was already tucked up in bed. The room at the other side looked good. A large hole in the ceiling had a dirty and creepy looking duvet half blocking it, half hanging down out of the hole. But apart from that, it was empty and most importantly had a fireplace. Not the best looking fireplace, but it appeared usable.

We'd made it, we were both relatively dry. We were pretty happy. Jay tried to shake my hand, I went instead for a high-five....a moment of confusion..."Sorry Jay, I couldn't see what you were doing" we laughed. I was blinded when he pointed his powerful bike light right into my face.

I rolled my bike through the front porch and around the corner and into the room, I was trying to be respectfully quiet, but the sleeping man possibly thought I was fighting off an angry bear.

Looking at the small pile of dry sticks left in the bothy we had a quick look around the back in case someone had left some larger fuel about. Nope, we'd have to go get some ourselves. Jay volunteered, "I'll go get some wood, do you fancy getting a brew on?". Much as that sounded good to me, the nearest wooded area was a distance away, back over the bridge and then along the loch side a way. "I'll come, we can carry more back, and get it done quickly." Maybe I was being helpful, or maybe I was just scared of the Ben Alder Cottage ghost.

The story goes that the last full-time resident of the bothy, McCook, the local gamekeeper, after living with his family in the cottage for forty years, one night climbed onto the table and hung himself from the rafters of the cottage. Since then, he has haunted the cottage, disturbing many a night's sleep.

Many visitors have reported strange noises, lights and an overpowering sense of unease and terrifying occurrences such as....in one terrifying instance.....a packet of digestives flying across the room.

Then there's the story of the woman who wails at night, grieving for the child she was forced to eat while being cut off in the cottage by snow storms for weeks.

These stories were most likely fabricated during the 20s and 30s when people started visiting the hills at weekends to escape the poverty of the great depression. The local landowners wanted to dissuade people from staying over in the empty cottage and so spread rumours of ghosts. In reality the gamekeeper, McCook, simply left the bothy and moved into a nearby town.

Yet another story tells of a walker who made his way to the bothy late in the day only to find the door locked from the inside.

105

After a bit of investigation he managed to open a window and tried to climb in. On swinging his first leg into the dark interior, he felt it being grabbed and pulled by some hands and then he felt some teeth sinking painfully in. He struggled to free his leg, kicking and pulling until he fell back out. Without stopping to look he took off across the boggy countryside until he felt safe to stop. Upon looking at his stinging leg there were deep teeth marks, like an animal with canines, clearly not human, yet whatever it was had hands to grip. The walker never went back. Maybe it was a monster?.......then again, maybe it was just someone with a dog who didn't want company?

After struggling across the bog and the bridge, and up wooded hillside, I found and then dragged back as many fallen branches as I could carry. Meanwhile, Jay cut some bigger logs off of a fallen tree and dragged those back. On reaching the bridge we took some time getting it all across before continuing on our way.

Finally, back in the cottage I started a fire (using my fire steel!). It lit easily enough, but it was hard work to get it going properly. I had to constantly blow while piling the slightly damp twigs on top. On one particularly strong blow, small embers became airborne and made their way right into my face. One stuck in the corner on my eyelid. I stood up and scrambled desperately to get the painful thing off me. Eventually it came off, leaving my eyelid very sore. Bloody fantastic. I asked Jay took a look "yep, you got a proper burn there, looks sore. Luckily it wasn't in your eye!". "Yeah, thanks, burning my face certainly is lucky!" At least the fire was now going strongly. I took the opportunity to change into some fresh, dry clothes.

We made some tea and then as we hadn't eaten a proper dinner, we shared a single packet of Supernoodles that I had taken as emergency food. For pudding we had more tea and shared some nice chocolate that Jay dug out of his bag. I kept my pork pie for the next day.

Somehow it was after 1.30am when we went to sleep on the floor in front of the now roaring fire. There was no ghostly activity, no phantasmal goings-on. The only thing which was metaphysical that night was the strong smell emanating from the socks and shoes drying in front of the fire.

I slept pretty well. A few times I was awoken by the cold after the fire had died down. My air mat seemed to be very slowly deflating. A couple of times when my body touched the cold floor I'd eventually gather up the energy to sit up and re inflate it. I've tested it since and can't find any leaks. Maybe McCook was making his presence known after all, by opening the valve while I was sleeping.

I awoke in the morning to a gloomily lit room. The view from my sleeping bag out the small window gave little clue as to how early it was. Looking at my watch I was surprised to see it was 9.30am. I hadn't slept this late for ages.

Starting a small fire to both warm ourselves and burn some rubbish, we heard some stomping about from outside of the room. "Morning!", the other occupant burst into the room. "Thought I had the place to myself last night, didn't think anyone would turn up as late as you guys!" We talked for a while, swapping tales of our routes in. He'd walked in from the north and had been planning to climb Ben Alder today. "I somehow managed to not bring any food!" he said, supping on the cup of soup he was holding. He noticed my quizzical look, "I found this packet of soup left behind by someone next door". "Don't suppose you have any food you can spare? I don't have anything else". We told of how we had little food ourselves, but I managed to spare a cereal bar anyway. Jay handed something over as well. I kept the pork pie. "Thanks, I'm just going to walk out of here today. Stupid trying to climb a hill with no food". And with that he was off.

I ate some granola for breakfast while we made some tea and packed up.

Walking out of the bothy, it was a revelation to see where it was situated. The loch was evidently quite high after the recent rains and wasn't that far from the front of the cottage. The surrounding mountains were covered in snow, but it hadn't been cold enough for snow at the level of the bothy. In fact it seemed warmer than the previous day. The frozen ground was a bit more

107

squidgy. Walking down to the loch I could look back to where we'd been the night before. I hadn't appreciated that we'd had to walk around a bay of sorts to reach the bothy. In the other direction the water stretched as far as I could see but a hillside blocked the view of the far end of the loch.

I took the mandatory bike-packing photo of our bikes leaning up against the bothy and then, it was time to go. We were planning to follow the side of the loch all the way to the north end, before turning and following cycle paths back down to the van at Pitlochry. We started out by following a path up the hill behind the bothy where we found a newish, well lain gravel covered path. This was a surprise, I'd expected to have to push again, but this was actually cycleable. It lasted about one kilometre. Then we were faced with a pedestrian gate, through a deer fence, which was altogether too small to fit our bikes through. We tried to squash a bike through the limited space between the swing gate and its outer structure. But it wasn't going to happen. Instead we had to pass our laden bikes between us over the eight foot high fence. From here on the path deteriorated. It was partly cycleable for another kilometre before the route became more heather and rock than path. The view was great though. We were traversing the side of a steep sided hill and as we moved onwards the view to the north opened out.

A long section of dragging, lifting and pushing our bikes followed. The GPS showed a marked path on the tiny map, but on the ground there was nothing which I'd describe as such. Eventually after passing through some young trees, getting whipped in the face by branches and then crossing a slippery ice covered stream, we climbed up the hillside a bit further and found a path of sorts. At least it was now possible to push. My back was aching from all the lifting.

Soon it became cycleable again. Jay leapt on and disappeared off down a hill. Apart from a few ditches, steep sections and boggy holes, we were now progressing quickly along the loch. Four kilometres later the steep hills flattened out and the landscape became greener. I reached a sign marked "McCooks Cottage". Next to it was the end of a track road. It was a relief, we still had a long way to go and we'd started off quite late. It was now almost lunch time and we'd come about seven kilometres. Jay was behind a bit and after a few minutes appeared over a hill and made his way down to the sign. "I need to stop for a minute. Had a bit of an awkward fall back there. I'm fine though....got away with it."

We were now opposite Corrievarkie Lodge, a previously abandoned house, which has fairly recently been done up as a self-catering getaway. Next to it we could see the small Ericht power station on the lochside, gravity fed from Loch Garry in the mountains above. I wasn't interested in the view though, "I'm knackered. I'm going to have an energy-gel". I usually carry a couple of gels when I'm out mountain biking, but generally the only time I use them is during races. If you've never had the pleasure then I'll describe them, they are foul tasting, super sweet, lightweight packets of a substance which will continue to emerge from previously consumed packets and will glue up whichever pocket you discard them in. They do, however, provide a quick surge of energy that can get you out of a tricky spot if you've forgotten to eat.....or like now, when you remembered, but just didn't have enough food to eat. I was still keeping my pie as something more substantial for later in the day. I chose a caffeinated gel for an extra boost. It did the job, a few minutes later I felt much better.

The track was easy to cycle and we quickly covered the next few kilometres to Ben Alder Lodge. This is a newly built 'Victorian' lodge built on the site of an old lodge by the new Swiss estate owners. We quickly passed by and continued on the now easy road. Apart from a short stop to fix Jay's front gear changing mechanism which had twisted during his earlier fall, we didn't have any trouble making our way along the loch side. The easy riding gave us a chance to appreciate the views.

Soon enough, we found ourselves approaching the village of Dalwhinnie. The track turned to tarmac and was supposed to get easier. However, in line with the rest of our short trip, this wasn't the case. The tarmac was covered in a layer of ice. We had to slow down considerably. Jay rode mostly along the middle of the road where there was slightly more grip provided by stones and plants sticking out through the ice. I stuck to the right-hand edge, it was bumpier but looked like there was more grip. Even so, every couple of minutes one of us would find our tyres sliding dramatically to the side. How we managed this section with neither of us actually falling is a mystery.

We reached the better roads of Dalwhinnie at about 1pm. Lunch time! After carefully crossing the slippery train tracks, and passing a very small man who was poking at the presumably frozen windscreen wipers on his huge old 4x4 with a broom handle, we were happy to have gotten the hardest section of today's ride out of the way. It was time for some lunch.

"Let's try the café" Jay suggested "Its got a proper wood fire!" To no-one's surprise the car park was empty, the blinds were drawn, it was closed. We continued down to the other option, the hotel on the main road. A sign outside informed us that the café within was also closed. "Bollocks" I'd been looking forwards to some hot food. "I going to eat the pork pie!" I said as Jay cycled off not particularly listening.

Across the road was a petrol station. On the sign outside it listed various amenities, one of which was 'Hot Food'. "Let's see what they've got" he shouted back.

Inside it was warm. I looked around to find the hot food consisted of various pies in a heated food display. We purchased a pie and hot coffee each and after a quick chat with the owner, we sat down on some stools at the table running along the front window. Now it may not sound brilliant, eating a pie that's been heated for who knows how long while sitting looking out a petrol station forecourt. But, the pie was amazing! I hungrily devoured it. It was delicious, the meat was tender and unlike normal cheap pies didn't contain any chewy bits or gristle. The pastry was crispy rather than soft and it took more force than expected to break through the thick, tasty crust. Jay considered having another. I too was tempted, but instead we bought some chocolate and other snacks before making our way out into the cold once again.

Setting off with some pie in my stomach, I was feeling good.

We cycled along a short section of road before turning off onto the 'Cycle Path to Pitlochry' as indicated by some spray paint on a large plinth made of cement and rocks which presumably at one time had a proper sign on it. I was disconcerted to see how covered in snow and ice the path was. We were just talking about it when I noticed we were heading for a giant, iced over puddle. I pulled on my brakes and slid to a stop, "Jay, you might want to stooooooop!" It was too late, he headed straight into the middle of the puddle, breaking through the ice on the way. For a moment it looked like he was going to keep going and make it all the way through, but as the ice slowed his progress, he toppled over onto his side. Only sticking his arm out to break his fall stopped him from being submerged.

He stood up and dragged his bike out of the water. It was less catastrophic than it looked. He had a wet lower leg and soaked glove and arm, but was otherwise fine. The dry-bags attached to his bike had mostly kept everything inside dry. Still, being even slightly wet in this relentless cold wasn't good. We continued on. The path wasn't as treacherous as it looked. The thin layer of snow atop the ice made it grippy enough. With some care on the corners and wooden foot bridges, we were fine apart from a couple of sketchy moments along the way where tyres slipped sideways.

We were now following a cycle path along the A9, one of the busiest roads in the country. I hadn't expected this part of the ride to be particularly nice. A few, thankfully short, times the path veered very close to the road. A couple of times the only thing between us and speeding lorries a few feet away was a thin crash barrier. At one point a lorry threw stones and rocks up as it passed. One hit Jay on the helmet. After this section, the route was surprisingly pleasant to cycle along. The path dropped down below the road next to the swollen river below. It made use of the old, practically abandoned, road. Down in the trees, there was little to no traffic noise. We covered the twenty kilometre length of the path quickly, riding by rapids and suspension footbridges, racing down wide, empty, tarmac while relaxing in the complete absence of traffic.

We reached a point where the path was blocked with barriers and a sign told it was closed. However, it provided no further explanation. The only alternative was to use the A9. The signs were pretty insistent that we don't use the path and the gates had been wired and chained shut. What was the reason for the closure we wondered? Flooding? Maybe the path had been washed away. Some maintenance, or other large machinery moving around perhaps? Most likely it was some kind of game shooting seeing as we were on the edge of some rather large estates. The cold would have driven the sizeable deer herds down from the mountains. "I think I'd rather take my chances on the path" I said lifting my bike over the fence and pushing through a gap. "Probably less chance of getting shot than run over by a lorry!" And so, after pausing to pump up a flat tyre caused by a very slow puncture on the other side of the gate, we continued on our way.

Further along, and the path was covered in ice once again, we passed a culvert, with water gushing out and passing just below the level of the road. But apart from these possible minor issues, there was no indication as to why it had been closed. We reached the far end of the section none the wiser.

Soon, the nice path ended and we switched onto the minor road for the last section back to Pitlochry. It was now getting dark and so, once again, we were riding with our failing lights. My front light was dimming, Jay's rear light had given up completely. He cycled in front, while I struggled to keep up given that I could no longer see the road properly. We were both knackered and now longed for the end. We reached the village of Blair Atholl where a welcome looking pub provided an excuse to stop and warm up with some coffee. After a quick stop and warm up in front of a lovely 'real flame' gas fire, we finished the last ten kilometres back to the van in Pitlochry. Dodging flooded sections of road the whole way.

We'd made it! Despite all the issues, I'd really enjoyed it, only the last few kilometres had been a struggle. Once changed into some warm, dry clothes, I sat in the front of the van as Jay drove back home…...and we ate the pork pie.

Outer Hebrides and Skye Route:

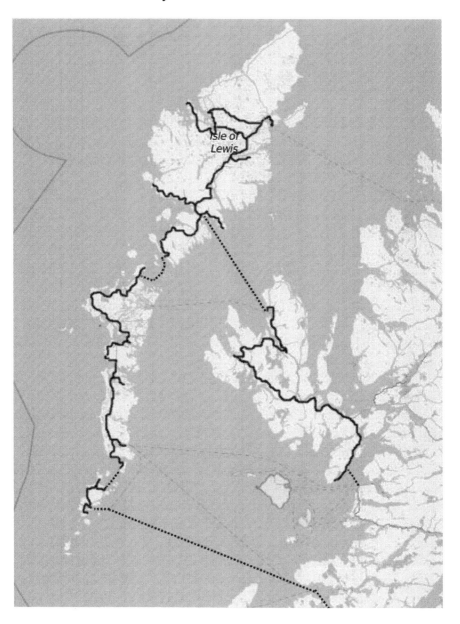

The Outer Hebrides and Skye

Al and I were once again on the move, and back on our way to Oban, the main Ferry terminal from which we could travel onwards to the western isles. We'd met in Glasgow before taking the final three hour train up to the coast.

This time we had a rough plan to visit the Outer Hebrides which neither of us had visited before. I'd looked at these islands many times on maps and thought about getting myself out to them, but somehow I'd never got around to it.

And so, on a grey misty day, we were once again, passing the time in Oban drinking coffee while waiting for the ferry to start loading. I read a guide book I'd bought as we waited.

The Outer Hebrides is a 220 kilometre long chain of 15 or so main islands (119 islands in all), separated from the mainland by the roughly 30-40 kilometre wide waters of the 'Minch'.

The Minch is where the storm kelpies, or blue men of the Minch, are rumoured to live. Supposedly, these things were of human form and had the power to create storms. They would approach boats and recite some lines of poetry to the skipper, who then had to complete the poem or the blue men would try to upturn the boat.....maybe a clever poet came up with the story to garner interest in his writings.

The stories may have originated from sightings of tattooed Picts (the main group of people living in the east and north of Scotland at the time) crossing the Minch in kayak style boats. Another possible source of the legends may have been the slaves of Vikings, who were taken here from North Africa. It's thought that these slaves were often Tuareg people of the Sahara, known for dressing from head to foot in blue. They were known as "the blue men of the desert". How they would have coped with the change in climate from dry, hot desert, to the freezing, sometimes hellish weather of the north of Scotland is anyone's guess.

On the islands, Gaelic is spoken widely as the predominant language, although this almost wasn't the case as 'the Education Act 1872' meant, that for generations, the islanders were forbidden to speak their native language in school. There are people to this day who remember being beaten for speaking Gaelic in the classroom.

Although the weather on the Islands is surprisingly mild for their position in the North Atlantic, it can be windy. The writer W.H.Murray famously said that if an islander is asked for the coming forecast "he will not, like a mainlander answer dry, wet or sunny, but quote you a figure from the Beaufort scale". In fact one day in six is measured as a gale at the Butt of Lewis, and after the worst storms fish can often be found on top of the 190m high Barra Head cliffs, having being blown there.

It was finally time to board the ferry and we did so in the usually way, strapping our bikes to the walls, this time along with quite a few other cyclists. After exploring the ferry, one of the largest to serve the islands of Scotland, I settled down in a comfy spot and continued reading.

Religion is still a strong influence on the most protestant Harris and Lewis, where everything shuts down on Sundays to the extent that even washing isn't hung out. One of the main religious sects is the Calvinist Free Church of Scotland. Which always sounds to me like some levity would be involved. But then the only Calvin I've ever come across is from reading Calvin and Hobbes cartoons. I couldn't be more wrong. Anyway, they are also known as the 'Wee Frees' (although they don't like this name). Both this lot, and the even stricter Free Presbyterian Church of Scotland (confusingly known as the 'Wee Wee Frees') are very conservative and don't go in for any decorations, ornaments or even music and singing in their churches.......clearly they don't have a marketing department.

I headed up to the deck at the front of the ship. We were still a long way off from the islands, I could see the outline of the low hills on the horizon as we ploughed through the white topped waves. The 'MV the Lord of the Isles' gently rocked as I stood on the forward deck watching the land grow larger and keeping an eye out for any wildlife.

After a while I'd had enough of the cold, and I met Al back indoors for some food. No big ferry journey is complete without having a helping of those special baked beans, which probably by some ancient sea-going decree by some high-ranking naval commander, must be heated for several days, concentrating the sauce and softening the beans, before being served to customers. I like them.

The ferry was headed for Barra, the second southernmost inhabited island in the chain. From here we'd be cycling north. After five hours, the ferry closed in on Castlebay, the main village on the island, and where we'd be getting off the boat. I started to get excited. It was an impressive bay with Kisimul castle, possibly the oldest standing castle in Scotland (1039), sitting on the rocks a short distance out in the water from the village. The houses and shops neatly lined the road from the slipway, with the largest hill on Barra, 'Heaval', sitting right behind.

We rolled off onto solid land and fought our way through the stressful traffic jam of about four cars, before heading south. It was already the middle of the afternoon and, as Barra isn't very big, we rode south for a few short kilometres to take a look at Vatersay, the most southernmost inhabited island in the chain. It's also the most westerly permanently inhabited place in Scotland.

The single-track road took us around the edge of an inlet running west of the main bay and giving us a view back over the town. The low sun burst through the clouds, turning the world a warm shade of autumnal orange. A further brief ride along the shoreline took us to the southern end of the island. Here it became obvious just how fractured the lands here are. There were rocky islands in every direction, the damp rock of the hillsides glinting in the bright light.

Cycling across a short 200 metre long man-made causeway

with the sea only a couple of feet away to either side, we reached the small island. The road connection was built in 1991, mostly to ease the passage of cattle to the renowned grazing land on the island. Before the causeway, the cows had to swim. The drowning of Bernie the prize bull while attempting the crossing in 1986 hastened the project...I'm not joking.

Continuing on down a tiny road on the east side we stopped by a stream which had some kind of wreckage strewn across it. Climbing down the hill to take a look it became clear that a plane had crashed. Bits of aluminium were scattered all over and some large bits were lying on the ground like it happened yesterday. Later on, I looked it up, I found out that in 1944 a Catalina flying boat, JX273, being used by the RAF on a training exercise had taken off from Oban fully loaded with depth charges under each wing, got lost and, flying too low, crashed into the hill above the road. Three were killed, but somehow there were six survivors. The wreckage was later dragged down the hill by the RAF and left at the side of the road.

We wandered back over the hillside through the heather towards our bikes. There's a purple flower here called 'shore bindweed' which doesn't grow anywhere else in Scotland. The story goes that it originated from seeds that Bonnie Prince Charlie took back from France and planted here. For once, this particular story about Charlie is actually probably true.

We visited the beach (named 'sand hole' on the map) and crossed to the southern end of the island. Vatersay is made up of two rocky hills with a sand bar connecting them. On a map it reminds me of the shape of a toffee being pulled into two, the middle being stretched perilously thin. A few houses were clustered together near the bottom end of the island where the road came to an end. We didn't hang around for long through. There wasn't much to see here at the end of the world. We spent a few minutes taking in the view before making our way back and returning across the causeway to Barra.

Our plan was to take a ferry north in the morning, so we had the rest of the day to explore Barra and find somewhere to camp for the night. We continued up the west side on the circular road. There were some amazing beaches here, lying between rocky outcrops. Beautiful, clean, white sand, backed by the low lying vegetation known as machair. This is a type of dune grassland, high in calcerific shell content, unique to these islands and parts of Ireland. They are of special interest due to their unique ecosystems including carpets of wild flowers and types of birds and bees which are rarely found elsewhere.

We found ourselves in the small settlement of Borve, or Borgh, depending on your map. Buildings were scattered along the floor of a deep valley heading inland. Even the numerous old vehicles left to decay here did little to diminish from the beauty of the place. The nearest scrap yard being a long ferry trip away means that properly disposing of old cars on these islands is difficult and expensive.

A couple of standing stones were in a field at the edge of the road. One was lying on the ground, the other looked like it would follow soon. "If they're not standing, they're just stones." said Al unimpressed, climbing back on his bike and cycling off.

Just to the north of the settlement was a beach even more impressive than those we'd seen earlier. Edged by dunes, the sand stretched away from the headland in a long curve.

We cycled on, into the light wind, before the road turned away from the sand and headed inland, passing a couple of modern looking houses with curved ends. Presumably these were designed to deflect the worst of the weather coming in off of the Atlantic.

As the sun set and darkness started to fall we set about looking for a place to camp for the night. We headed up a small road at the north end of the island which took us on to the Eoligarry peninsula. It's sometimes said that the island of Barra is shaped like a turtle swimming north. A rounded flipper at each corner and the peninsula being the neck and head at the top. I'm not convinced of the description. If someone had shown me a painting this shape and described it as a turtle, I'd have hoped they were less than 2 years old and not a renowned artist.

118

We climbed up a gentle hill for several kilometres, the landscape becoming rockier as we went. The wind was picking up and the temperature was dropping as we reached the highest point and rolled back down to the shore on the other side. We turned a corner and before us opened out a huge, flat, shallow bay, wet from the receding tide. This was the site of the famous Barra airport. Unique as it's apparently the only one where scheduled flights use the beach as a runway. There are three runways marked out with wooden posts on the beach in a triangle, allowing planes to always land into the wind. Except, of course, when the tide is in. We pushed on, the road following the bay's edge. Half way around there is the incongruous sight of a modern looking air traffic control tower standing next to a tiny passenger terminal on the very edge of the beach. We passed behind it.

Leaving the road and following the edge of the beach around, we found a nice spot to stop for the night (off of the main beach, in case of unexpected flights!). It was getting late by now, and I was glad to get the tent up and settle into cooking some dinner while watching the light fade.

I made some well-deserved pasta and a nice tomato based sauce with broad beans. We followed this off with some, almost compulsory when camping, whisky. I zipped up my jacket and lay back on the machair wishing the sky was clearer. It was so dark that were it cloudless, the stars would have been spectacular. It had been a pretty good first day.

Day 2

I woke early and cooked up some bacon for breakfast on my trusty old Triangia stove. It may have been heavy, big, almost completely uncontrollable, and dangerous, what with it basically being of a small tin can filled with burning, sloshing, meths which burns with an impossible to see invisible flame, and which can only be controlled by very carefully putting a piece of metal on top to partially cover the opening.......but it did the job. We were shortly enjoying bacon rolls. Shortly after that, I wasn't enjoying scraping layers of congealed fat off of the pan without the help of hot water. Frying anything while wild camping is always a mistake.

The beach was partly covered in water. It looked like I wouldn't get to see any planes landing. We packed up and soon headed off towards the Aird Mhor ferry terminal. We were late as usual...according to the timetables we'd collected in Oban, and so cycled furiously along. We had to be careful though as while cyclists technically can't be stopped by the police for speeding, they technically can be stopped for "Furious cycling" under an obscure law from 1847. Many cyclists cite that being caught for this is one of their life ambitions.

We made it to the lonely terminal to find the ferry hadn't yet arrived. There was nothing here but a few cars, a signpost showing the ferry times with a pulsating red LED display, and a small toilet building. Soon enough the boat silently appeared from behind the protective harbour wall and laboriously made its way towards us.

Rolling down the ramp, we joined ten or so cars for the forty minute trip across to the next island in the chain, Eriskay. I climbed up to the outer deck. I watched as a ferryman lifted the ferry ramp and we slid away. Now that we'd stopped exerting ourselves, the cold wind whipping across the water and seemingly unimpeded by my light cycling clothes, was gnawing at my insides. After a few minutes of watching the ferry manoeuvring, I headed down into the tiny waiting room in search of warmth. I was surprised to find there was even a shower, I was quite tempted to retrieve my towel from my panniers.

The ferry unloaded and the cars disappeared up the only road. Eriskay is small, about two kilometres wide and three long, and is probably most famous as the island where the real Whisky Galore episode took place. In 1941 the SS Politician ran aground on its way to Jamaica with a cargo of Whisky and famously it was raided by the islanders and relived of most of its load of 24,000 boxes of whisky, hiding the haul from the excise men who came looking. What is less well known is that there was also about 300,000 ten-shilling notes, worth several million today. Two-thirds of this was salvaged by the boat owners, but a substantial amount went missing and later kept turning up in circulation around the world.

Cycling on through the sparsely situated houses and over the 1.5 kilometre long causeway which led from Eriskay to the much larger island of South Uist, the sea was a crystal green and shallow enough to see the sandy bottom. If someone had shown me a photo of it I'd probably of guessed it was of the Caribbean.

We continued along the main road. To be fair there wasn't a whole lot of choice. The road led us through the dandelion filled fields northwards towards the tiny hamlet of Dalibrog. Small causeways carried the road through the many small lochans which dotted the amazing landscape.

A co-op provided an opportunity for a break from pedalling and to resupply, before we decided to take a detour along a side road to the east coast to the main town on the island, Lochboisdale.

The wind was starting to get stronger and blew us along as we made our way along the road all the way across to the other side of the island. The road was sparsely lined with houses all the way. I guess when there are relatively few people and plenty of space, why not have some space between the buildings. Eventually, we reached the coast at the far side and after having a look around we went up the hotel situated just next to the slipway, on a rocky hill looking out to sea. We leant our bikes against a wall, and while Al dug out the maps I went inside to buy some drinks.

It was very dark inside the hotel, but I found the bar and after some confusion, with us wanting to go outside, and being told that we had to stay inside the bar if we wanted food, we settled into a table near a window to enjoy the sunny view from our cold and dark position.

Lochboisdale juts out into a sheltered bay, Loch Baghasdail. It expanded from a few remote houses in the 19th century when it became a fishing station during the herring boom. The pier was built in 1880 to allow steamers to stop off here.

The herring boom started when the British Government put a bounty of £3 per ton on herring boats over 60 tons, plus an extra bonus for any herring that was sold abroad. This, the advent of fast steamships, and the railways, meant that the fishermen could sell the fish more easily and hence they set out to maximise their catches.

The bounty was initiated as the Government were worried that the Dutch were dominating the market with their large boats, called buses.

The industry grew from a local, seasonal one, and the boats began to follow the herring shoals around the British coast, taking with them an army of curers, merchants and the herring lasses, who gutted and packed the fish. It must have been a strange existence for the onshore workers, but there was good money to be made.

Unfortunately, there wasn't any herring on the lunch menu in the hotel, but I had some pretty nice haddock and chips, and a fine pint of local-ish ale from the Hebridean Brewing Company.
Soon we had to leave, and after adjusting to the bright sun, once again our wheels were spinning. With a choice of one road, we returned the way we had come, due west across the island, back to the main road and straight into the wind. It was slow progress until,

finally, we took a right and continued north for a relatively easy twenty kilometres. Although this was the main (and only) road up the island, cars were few and far between. It was also quite flat on this side of the island. We rode on, admiring the view of the sea and machair on one side, lochans and sizeable hills on the other.

The road turned into a single-track with passing places. Wanting to see a bit more of the island we took another right up a smaller road. Al wanted to take a look at the Loch Druidibeag national reserve, an area of mountains, peat bogs and moorland and a haven for much of the best wildlife. Shortly after turning off, we were surrounded by small wild ponies. Some were oblivious, but a couple seemed quite inquisitive and came over for a closer look. I tried to find out, but I don't think these were the famous Eriskay ponies, related to the original native ponies. They were used by crofters for moving peat and seaweed around and are now rare as there are only about 500 left in the world.

We climbed on up to the highest point of the road and stopped for a break in a large lay-by. While I was digging around in a pannier for some food a small mini-bus pulled up right next to me. It stopped about a foot away, vibrating noisily. "What the hell?...why do they have to stop here..right next to us..in the middle of nowhere?" I thought to myself, slightly annoyed. The door opened with a swish. A group of pensioners alighted and flocked around me.
"Hello...sorry about parking right next to you, we didnae want to drive into the potholes you see?"
"Ahh...no problem", I said, my annoyance instantly dissipating.
"We're on a birdwatching trip. Have ye seen anything interesting on yer trip?"
We chatted for a while. I turned down their offer of some tea out of a battered old tartan flask. Eventually they drifted off to look at the view from the other end of the lay-by, taking out an assortment of binoculars to scan the landscape. I joined Al who was sitting up on some elevated, flat rocks. We watched the gaggling flock of old folks. After a time they re-boarded the bus. With twenty people waving out the window and a sputter from the exhaust, they slowly

disappeared off down the hill. In the other direction, we watched clouds drifting across the distant mountains of Skye.

Rolling back down the hill we passed the horses again and then continued up the main road.

Further on, we saw a nine metre tall statue up on the hill to our right. This is 'Our lady of the Isles' built in protest at the proposed militarisation of the island in the 50s. Today it stands beneath a radar tracking station for the nearby missile testing range which is part of the same system monitored by another radar station based on St Kilda.

This area has come to be known as the place 'where religion meets radar'.

The author Compton Mackenzie, who wrote the book 'Whisky Galore' about the shipwreck full of whisky, wrote a sequel of sorts, called 'Rockets Galore' about this area. It wasn't as commercially successful as it predecessor, although it was also made into an 'Ealing comedy' film. Many of the characters from the original book returned, this time unhappy at the disruption to their lives the new rocket base would create. So they set out to impede the construction. The film was panned. Reviewers wrote that the best thing about the movie was the images of the lovely island scenery shot in the relatively new colour film format.

To the west of the road are the three launch areas, and a huge circular area which was used for antenna arrays. This area was used in the late fifties to test the Corporal missile. This was the first guided nuclear missile and was built in a UK-US collaboration. Also, the first unmanned aircraft to cross the Atlantic landed here on South Uist in 1998. The range was also used for the first missile test firings from the Eurofighter Typhoon, the nearby Benbecula airport getting upgraded to support the tests.

The guide book gave a good review of a seafood restaurant near the top end of the island. So again we took a detour, and sought it out. Along the tiny road we passed a junction with a statue of the Virgin

124

Mary standing inside a glass box. This reminded me of the wayside shrines encountered throughout Italy which vary between simple wooden crosses, elaborate niches in walls, towers, caves and small buildings. They are often found along pilgrim routes, land boundaries or were erected as memorial to a dead person. This particular shrine felt out of place here but was a reminder that these islands at the southern end of the chain were predominantly Catholic.

Soon enough we found it, the Orasay Inn. It was an unassuming building. We went in and made ourselves at home with a pint and I was glad to see herring and potatoes on the menu. I ordered them. It was pretty good.

Soon enough, we headed back down the road and, after stopping to take a photo, crossed the long causeway, with its famous "Caution: otters crossing" signposts at either end. We were now on the island of Benbecula, squashed between South and North Uist. It was getting late and so, looking at the map, and hoping for a nice shower, we headed for a proper campsite which was nearby in the stretched out village of Liniclate. We set up our tents in the Shell Bay camp-site, with a view of a nearby wind turbine spinning majestically. It was now dark and after sorting out my things inside the tent, I ate some biscuits, climbed into my cosy sleeping bag and fell instantly asleep.

Day 3

I awoke in the pitch black, with the tremendous noise of heavy rain battering the outside of the tent. I lay there, trying to get back to sleep, wondering if the weather would continue into the next day. There's something comforting about being in a tent in the rain. Something about the dichotomy between your current level of comfort and what it would be like to be the other side of the thin material currently protecting you. The noise itself is relaxing, it seems to distract your brain from whatever else was bothering you. In fact you can download recordings of rain on a tent to help you sleep when at home. Although, if you want a more realistic experience you should also put some damp, smelly socks near your head, and use a jumper as a pillow.

The morning arrived far too soon, but the thought of a hot shower got me out of bed. Soon, I was fully awake and much cleaner. Unfortunately, I then had to put on the same dirty cycling clothes again. Still, I'd learnt from experience that it was far better to travel light than to carry too much spare clothing.

Al was up as well, and we had some breakfast and coffee. One luxury I've started taking on trips is a small moka pot to make coffee. It doesn't weigh much or take up much room and as I like black coffee anyway, it doesn't require milk to be carried. There are lighter plastic options designed specifically for travelling, but moka pots can be put directly on top of a camping stove. There's something satisfying about waiting for the little pot to start steaming while otherwise roughing it in a tent. Coffee and cycling for some reason go very well together.

Caffeine was once on the World Anti-Doping Agency's list of controlled substances (the limit was the equivalent of about eight espresso shots per day) as its known to boost cycling performance. So professional cyclists had to be careful. In studies of high intensity physical activity its found to increase the time until exhaustion.

Personally, I like it as I'm not really a morning person. Frankly anything that help me wake up properly can't be bad.

We set off on the ten kilometre road across Benbecula. The wind was getting stronger. Near the end of the road we passed close to Benbecula airport before starting out on the exposed five kilometre arc of road which links across a sandy, tidal bay to the island to North Uist. First we cycled the thin causeway across to the tiny stepping stone island of Grimsay and then over a further causeway across to North Uist. Grimsay may be tiny, but, thanks to the shellfish industry, it has a thriving little harbour at the sheltered settlement of Kallin. Mostly the small fleet of colourful boats catch scallops, lobsters and prawns. The quality of the catch is so good that Spanish trucks come directly here to buy product for restaurants back home. Its also a base for boat building and repairs. A handy sign above the harbour told of diverse wildlife to be found out in the shallow waters between the islands.

As we slowly rolled across the island the sun burst out from behind the thick cloud, but it was still cold in the wind.

North Uist is stark. The landscape is mostly made up of low lying peat bog and lochans. The island, although the largest of the islands we'd crossed so far, felt ephemeral, like it was slowly being overwhelmed by water and beginning to sink. The lack of hills and trees added to the other-worldly feel.

We plodded on as the wind increased. With nothing to shelter us and no alternative route options we could do nothing but to ride straight into it. Many times I've been involved in the recurring cyclist's conversation about the frustration of having to cycle into the wind, expending more energy at the same time as moving more slowly. I think I used to be the same but I've tired of letting myself be bothered by it, and learned just to expect it as part of the experience. However, this was different. The wind really was insane. We took turns cycling at the front while the other got at least a little shelter behind. We were taking a long time to cover the kilometres. It was sapping my morale.

Stopping behind a wall for a few minutes to get some shelter, my legs cramped up as I got off my bike. "Pain is just weakness leaving the body" Al commented. I must have been weaker than I thought.

We cycled through miles of moorland and bog, leaning forwards on our handlebars in an attempt to minimise our forward facing, wind battered, profiles. We passed a few areas where people were digging for peat. The dark blocks having been piled in a specific neat pattern to aid with drying, while allowing the any rain to run off the tops. Small holes or ditches showed that this wasn't a commercial operation, but just the locals gathering fuel for their fires using traditional methods.

Usually starting in May, sections of peat are cut using a peat iron ('tairsgeir' in Gaelic). This is a long wooden handle with a metal blade attached at right-angles at one end. There's a step on one side of the handle to allow extra pressure to be applied with a foot when cutting.

We stopped at a perfectly placed café by the side of the road which was a product of diversification in a place of so few customers; it was also the school, and shop, and library. I ordered a coffee and chocolate cake and sat down with a magnificent view out to sea. I was just glad to be out of the wind for a bit. The coffee and cake were excellent! A few other locals were milling about. This was the first place where I noticed everyone was chatting to each other in Gaelic. The only Gaelic I know is 'Ciamar a tha Sibh?' pronounced (Ky-mer a ha shiv) which means 'How are you?' I've no idea why this phrase has stuck in my head when lots of other possibly more useful stuff has long been forgotten. And if I ever deployed this phrase I'd have no idea what the answer meant. I do also know that Scottish Gaelic should be pronounced 'gaa-lik' rather than 'gay-lik' which is confusingly the English for Irish Gaelic.

Eventually, we had to leave and continued our battle with the wind all the way up the west coast. A few hours later, we were bored with the monotony of cycling along the main road. 'It looks like there's a nature reserve' Al said examining the map as the wind did its best to destroy it. 'Let's take a look'.

We took a short detour along a smaller road to have a look at the Balranald RSPB nature reserve. All the birds were hiding from the wind. I don't think I saw a single bird, but it was certainly a beautiful bay. Before me was an oval stretch of water, opening out to the sea at one end, and surrounded by sandy beach. Behind the beach were grassy hillocks, presumably sand dunes, covered in short vegetation. The water was strikingly blue, even though the surface was choppy. I climbed over a dune and, sheltered from the wind, I sat down for a rest. In autumn the bay is a major stopping point for huge flocks of barnacle geese as they return from Greenland. There's also a healthy population of otters which can occasionally be seen. Not today though.

After a look around the visitor centre and a very scenic nearby cemetery, it was time to head back inland. Thankfully, the wind was now no longer head on. We didn't have any food left and so when we came across the ubiquitous co-op in the sparse settlement of Solas, we dumped our bikes and went to buy something for our tea. There was a small sheltered area with picnic tables opposite and we took the opportunity to have a break and eat some cakes and crisps.

Shortly after, we got going once again and passed an old traditional thatched house, whitewashed, with peat stacked up outside. I stopped to take some photos. It must have been a hard life for earlier islanders, living off the land in this storm battered environment.

We took the turn off to the north and cycled up and over another causeway, this time onto the small isle of Berneray (confusingly, the most southerly island in the outer Hebrides chain is also called Berneray.)

The ferry which we needed to take left from a slipway at the north end of the causeway, but we had some time to spare before the next one was due and so we continued on up the three kilometre long coast road. Through the small settlement of Borgh there was a bay with plenty of rocks and on those rocks some seals flopped around or slept.

There were lots of ruins of houses along the roadside. The people of these islands were particularly hard hit by the clearances of 1849. The local landowners, the MacDonalds, ruled over the locals like spoilt kings. As people became more civilized and started relying on the law to sort out disputes rather than violence, the loyal people were no longer required by the landowners to fight in battles with neighbouring clans. Also, the local kelp industry (burning seaweed to create ash which was then sold off as an ingredient to be used in many processes, including iodine production) was failing. Demand for the kelp products was dying down as other sources of ingredients were found. At the same time as this, the landowners were raising rents. But the hardy locals could probably have survived all this. What really did it for the locals was the introduction of sheep. The MacDonalds cleared the people living on the land and their crofts to make room for more profitable sheep grazing. Those who refused to leave were evicted with force, sometimes with brutal methods.

Racism also played a part, some influential books of the time argued that the Celtic race was inferior to the Anglo-Saxon race, and said they were to blame for the weak economies of the Highlands.

A leading Edinburgh newspaper (which is still going today), wrote "Collective emigration is, therefore, the removal of a diseased and damaged part of our population. It is a relief to the rest of the population to be rid of this part".

The beach at the end of the track was amazing, and sheltered from the worst of the wind. We had it to ourselves. In 2009 photos of the beach on the other side of the island were inadvertently used in advertising for Kae Bae beach in Thailand. Someone tasked with creating the adverts just grabbed some nice looking beach pictures from the internet. Understandable, given the white sands and azure seas. Bit nippier though.

Although the sands of the photo look tranquil, in 1697 the wind whipped them up enough to completely bury the nearby settlement of Siabaidh. It's thought that the original buildings are still buried somewhere beneath the sand, waiting to be excavated by future archaeologists. Nearby, a forest of submerged willow and birch tree stumps have been found below the high tide mark.

On our return down the road we still had some time to spare. We decided to spend it in the Lobster Pot tea rooms, refuelling with tea and scones.

Soon enough it was time for the ferry. The islands aren't far apart, but the sea route to Leverburgh on Harris to the north is shallow, particularly rocky and full of small islands. This forces the boat to take a long, indirect, and winding route. In fact the ferry had to be specially designed with apparatus to allow it to be more manoeuvrable.

The hour long trip gave me time to rest my legs, I was looking forwards to stopping for the night. It was busy inside the passenger waiting rooms so I climbed up to the deck at the front of the boat to watch as we made our way through the choppy sea. Plumes of spray were leaping off the front of the detracted loading ramp and sweeping across the railings. I found a great spot next to a tall exhaust funnel, which both sheltered me from the wind and spray, and provided heat. Soon I was joined up on the deck by Al as we watched the sun dappled hills of South Harris get closer.

We were now about half-way up the chain of islands in terms of distance. We were heading towards by far the largest of the islands in the chain, in fact it was the largest island in Scotland.

Rolling off the boat and up the large concrete ramp, we found ourselves in a small industrial site just as it started to rain. As there was a small pub called 'the Anchor' to the side of the pier it seemed rude not to go in. We ordered some beer and lingered in the warm surroundings watching the rough sea, and the rain bouncing off the ground outside the window. After a while, the clouds thinned out, the world brightened, and the rain stopped. We headed out to find somewhere to camp for the night.

Already feeling tired, the pint pushed me over the edge. I managed to keep up with Al as the road passed through the settlement right along the water's edge. But as the road headed up a not very steep incline, my legs gave up. It was a real struggle to keep going, all I wanted to do was lie down at the side of the road and not move for several hours. Each turn of the cranks took enormous effort. I was feeling light headed and for a while hated my bike, the weight I was carrying, the fact that Al never seemed to get tired.

Eventually, after a long fight to not give up, I made it to the top of the hill. Al was a way down the road, rolling off into the distance. I stopped for a few minutes and dug out an emergency Snickers bar, before devouring it.

I got back on and concentrated on slowly pushing on the pedals with my head down. A few kilometres later and I was already feeling much better. The chocolate bar had done its job.

The road skirted a bay between the hilly peninsula on Toe Head and the steep sided hills behind. To the left of the road the sandy bay stretched for miles. We stopped and climbed over some dunes and found a great sheltered camping spot on some machair in between. I was very happy to have stopped for the day. I set up my tent, threw everything inside and set up the stove for cooking. The light was fading and we ate quickly before heading to bed.

Day 4

The next morning, we woke to the all too familiar sound of rain pattering on the outside of the tents. I went back to sleep. It was 10 o'clock before I struggled awake and unzipped the door to find the rain had stopped. We were camped on the edge of Scarastabeg beach, surrounded by sandy hillocks. Short grasses were doing their best to hang on in the unstable environment.

The shifting of the dunes here recently revealed an ancient inhumation burial. This is where a hole is dug before the deceased is placed in and covered in rocks. When examined, much of the body was found intact. There's likely more hidden under the dunes. Luckily, I didn't see any feet sticking out of the sand as I made my way down through the dunes towards the sea. I emerged out on to the flat hard sand of the bay. The tide was out so the sand stretched for miles. I walked for a while down to the water. There was noticeably little sea weed or other debris on the beach. It was as if it had been cleaned earlier that morning. There was no-one else about. Even Al was still back at his tent. I had one of the most beautiful beaches I think I've seen, all to myself.

An hour and a half later, and with everything re-packed into my panniers. We set off up the road. At first we followed the coast, watching as the large waves, created somewhere out in the vast Atlantic, crashed in against the rocky shoreline, bursting up again in a last show of power before their death. I was feeling much better this morning and after looking at the map I was actually excited at the thought of going over some proper mountains.

The road turned away from the sea and cut across the interior of South Harris before turning north again. The mountains reared into the sky ahead of us. An imposing sight.

Then, with no houses anywhere to be seen, we passed a

large black and white dog standing in the middle of the road. Apart from a quick acknowledgement of our existence, he didn't take any notice of us and appeared to be deep in thought. We passed by.

This stark boulder covered landscape looked otherworldly, like nothing I'd seen anywhere else. In fact it's so strange, it was used in the Stanley Kubrick film "2001: A Space Odyssey". They filmed from small low-flying planes and then tinted the captured images as a stand in for the surface of Jupiter.

We rolled into the main town on Harris, Tarbert. The name comes from the Norse word 'tairbeart', which means crossing point, or portage. This is why there are at least 13 other places in Scotland which confusingly share the name. All situated between two nearby waterways which the Vikings used to drag their boats between. This particular Tarbet is now the terminal for the ferry to Uig on Skye.

Vikings first appeared on these islands about 700AD, firstly raiding and then settling in the decades which followed. Ketill Flatnose was one the first prominent figures. Mr Flatnose accumulated a huge realm on the islands and made alliances with many of his neighbouring Viking leaders. Although, in theory they were supposed to be controlled by the Norwegian Crown, in reality they were too remote and could do as they pleased.

I didn't know this before looking it up in the guide book but in 1098 the Hebrides became officially Norwegian after (the boringly named) Edgar of Scotland decreed they be handed to Magnus Barefoot of Norway. Magnus was finally accepted by the locals as the King after he showed his personal power by also taking control (by fighting the current Viking leaders) of Orkney and the Isle of Man. He was brutal. His skald (personal poet) with the descriptive name of Bjorn Cripplehand wrote, presumably with his good hand:

In Lewis Isle with fearful blaze,
The house-destroying fire plays.
To hills and rocks the people fly,

134

Fearing all shelter but the sky.

The Outer Hebrides remained Norwegian until 1266 when, worried about the stability of the Western Isles, the current King, Haakon Haakonsson, set off to intimidate the Scots into backing off. Unfortunately for him, the canny Scots deliberately prolonged negotiations until the weather was too bad for the King to leave. He was forced to wait it out on Orkney, became ill, and died. The islands were returned officially to Scotland a couple of years later.

We took a look around and I bought some more unhealthy snacks and supplies before continuing northwards up the main road. And into the first proper hills of the trip. They didn't start gently. The first hill was a sharp, steep climb from sea-level to 150m. The gradient lessened thereafter as we rode on slowly climbing through the first valley.

Soon enough, we reached the far end, to see that we were about to reap the reward for all that climbing. The road could be seen ahead, curving around the hillside, before continuing onwards northwards. All downhill. I looked at my speedometer on my handlebars as we rolled down. As Al disappeared off in front with his skinny high-pressure tyres I decided I wouldn't bother pedalling to keep up. I still hit the fastest speed of the trip. A heady 40km/h.

It was fairly easy riding for the next ten kilometres along the edge of Loch Shiphoirt. The landscape was one of snow-poles marking the edges of the road, the occasional sheep grid, and new tree plantations on the hill sides.

We passed a sign "Failte do dh'Eilean Leodhais", or "Welcome to the Isle of Lewis". Strangely, we hadn't crossed a causeway or taken a ferry. Instead a tiny stream marks the boundary between the Harris and Lewis.

It's more the uniquely differing characters of the north and south areas of the same island which separate Harris and Lewis. Harris is hilly and rocky whereas Lewis is flat and peat covered. We still had some undulations to conquer before reaching the fully "Lewis" landscape. It was also time for lunch. We could have had a roadside picnic as for once we had enough supplies. A quick look at the map showed a tempting pub. It was a detour along a side road and of course it was up a hill, but seemed the better option.

A few kilometres later and, out of breath, we reached the Loch Erisort Inn. It was a good choice, the owner didn't seem at all bothered by our slightly obnoxious state of damp stinkiness and asked about our trip. He dispensed a couple of nice ales from behind a pinewood bar that looked better suited to a touristy beach resort than a pub on a remote heather covered island. The food we'd ordered was good as well. Hot and good sized portions, just what we were after.

The bar was adorned with old photos of the island. And piles of books about the area lay on the tables and around the fireplace. I picked up a book about peat production and was surprised to learn that even now, when you buy a house on Lewis, you are almost always allotted a small area of peat which is yours to extract and use. Although, this area will not necessarily be anywhere near your house!

Also, I learnt that the thick orange fibres (called "calcas") found in the extracted peat bricks were, in the past, often pulled out and smoked in place of tobacco.

I took my damp shoes off...luckily no-one else was in to complain. Although I'm sure the owner had disappeared into the back and was on the phone ordering up a large case of Febreeze. Or possibly checking if his insurance was in order before planning how best to burn the place to the ground.

Full of food and beer, we trundled back down to the main road and headed north once again. The landscape was flattening out now. Lochans became abundant as the rocks were replaced by miles of peat. After wiggling its way through a particularly dense area of lochans, the road became straighter, nothing more impeding its progress. This also meant that there was nothing to impede the wind and as it grew stronger my legs were once again flagging. A petrol station after a particularly long and boring straight section provided some Coke and a short break before we cycled the last few kilometres into Stornoway.

It was disconcerting to ride into the first proper town for a week. Cars and people which back in my home city of Edinburgh would fade into the background, took full command of my attention. We knew there was a camp-site here but we didn't really know where it was. After going the wrong way we were presented opportunity of visiting a big supermarket. It wasn't passed up. Hiding the bikes and locking them with an ineffective cable lock, we headed in to buy a load of supplies as well as replenishing our supply of whisky. Al placed a small bottle of rum on the checkout for good measure. We may have overdone it. Even after stuffing the panniers we still had a couple of heavy bags of shopping. We somehow managed to affix them to our bikes.

A large map on a pedestrian street showed the way to the holiday park. A short ride down a quiet lane later and we arrived at the camp-site reception. I looked at the price list while waiting for the owner to appear. It was a bit of a bargain at only £7 for a tent if you have a car.

"Hello, are you together, got a car?" a gruff voice said as a man appeared. Repressing the urge to state the obvious about my helmet and cycling clothes and the fact that the reception overlooked the completely empty, but for two bikes, entrance way, "No we're on bikes, just two separate small tents please?"

"That'll be £20".

"But it says £7 for each tent?"

"Yes, well it's not"

This was rapidly becoming farcical. I looked to Al for some help. He rolled his eyes and wandered out the door and left me to it.

"But that makes no sense, why is it cheaper if you have a car?"

The man seemed not to understand my problem and just shrugged.

"So how about we just pretend we have a car that will take up more space and make more mess driving over the grass and we call it £14?". He looked at me like I was the idiot, then "Noooooo......£20!"

I paid up, I was too tired to fight the lunatic any more, or look for somewhere else to camp.

I set my tent up on a soft looking patch of grass and without unpacking my sleeping mat and bag, lay down inside for a rest. What seemed like a few moments later Al appeared. "I think we should go out for some food. Maybe an Indian?" He appeared to have showered and put on some clean clothes while I had slept for almost an hour. "Yeah, that sounds good" I got up and looked at my watch. "Where are the showers?"

Half an hour later, after donning my semi-clean lightweight trousers, we zipped up the tents and headed off back into town on our bikes. No longer held back by the huge weight of our luggage, it was so easy to cycle back up the hill into town. My bike felt twitchy and responsive as we took a look around the small town centre while keeping an eye out for somewhere to eat. Soon enough, we found an Indian called the "Balti house" and went in.

Stornoway, set around a natural harbour, is the largest town of the Outer Hebrides with a population close to 10,000. It was settled by Vikings in the 9th Century. Nowadays it's still a busy harbour with a ferry link to the mainland and a small fishing fleet. Angus MacAskill (more of which later), the "strongest man who ever lived", lived here for a while before emigrating to Canada.

Filled with several beers and too much spicy food and having firmed up a plan for the next part of our trip, we headed off to our tents.

Day 5

We had a bit of a lie in the next morning and didn't get up until late. I felt like a different person. Maybe I hadn't been eating enough, or just needed an extra couple of hours of sleep, but I'd woken up feeling great. Unfortunately, the midges, so far missing from our current adventure, had appeared and were ravenous. We needed to escape from them. After a light breakfast, we quickly packed and heaved our heavy bikes back to an upright position. Our only restriction on this trip was that we had to be back home for work on a certain day. That day was in five days' time. We planned to spend two more days on Lewis and Harris and then take the ferry back over to Skye for the last couple of days, before catching the train south. We opted to head across to the west coast of Lewis to see probably the most famous attraction; the Callandish standing stones. This would mean missing out on exploring the huge top section of Lewis. Maybe another time.

The road to the west was amazing. What was marked on the map as an 'A' road, or a major road, turned out to be a quiet single-track across the flat peat-lands. Soon enough we turned onto an even smaller road marked on the map as 'Pentland Road'. This was much the same, maybe with a few more potholes. This road was almost dead straight as it gently climbed up towards the middle of the island. Originally, it was planned to build a railway line from Stornoway to the west coast to allow for easy and quick transportation of fish catches. However, although some initial planning and a rough, peaty track road was made along the route, it never reached fruition. This project is often attributed to Lord Leverhulme, but for once the failure wasn't his. It was well before his ownership of the land. Eventually, a proper road was built in 1912 along the route instead and named after John Sinclair, commonly known as Lord Pentland, who secured the funding for it.

For the first time ever, Al started complaining of a pain in his knees. I was surprised, usually it was me that suffered while he disappeared off into the distance. He took some ibuprofen and soon enough, once it had kicked in, he was back to normal.

The road ended near the west coast of the island at the hamlet of Carloway. We took a small diversion to the nearby Gearrannan blackhouse village. Leaving our bikes attached to a fence in the small car park we headed down the hill on foot. The village is made up of nine traditional crofting houses with their dry-stone and earthen walls and thatched roofs. Particularly distinctive are the ropes stretched over the thatch with heavy rocks tied onto the ends. These help stop the fierce Atlantic winds from destroying the roof.

These were the last inhabited blackhouses of the western isles and were finally abandoned in the early seventies due to the amount of work required to maintain them and the lack of basic facilities.

In 1989 the local community bought the houses and have since restored them using traditional methods. I was surprised to see that most of the houses are now available to rent for holidays and have been cleverly updated with discreet modern facilities. A few are maintained as they once would have been and can be visited.

Back on our bikes, we continued on down the coast road to the south. A couple of kilometres on, and next on our itinerary for what was becoming 'archaeology day' was a visit to the best preserved broch in the Outer Hebrides at Dun Carolway. We again locked the bikes up before climbing the steep hill up to the broch. The walls of which still reach up about ten metres, which meant we could go inside and climb up the still existing staircase to the top. Apparently, this structure is thought to date back to somewhere between 100BC and 100AD. After exploring, I sat in the sun in front of the broch to read a leaflet about it while enjoying a rare can of sugary Coke.

A bus load of tourists temporarily spoiled the peace. They all piled off of the bus excitedly taking photos of the broch, before re-boarding. I don't think a single one of them bothered to climb the hill to actually take a proper look. The bus sat with the engine noisily, and pointlessly, idling for ten minutes, before pulling away.

It was also time for us to make a move. The clouds were getting thicker anyway. We were very low on supplies, so were hopeful of finding a shop of some sort along the way. At the very least we knew there was a café at our next stop.

We returned to the main road and continued south the ten km towards the famous Calanais Standing stones (and café!).

Al's creaking knees returned and were clearly bothering him as he fell behind even my sedate pace. But we pushed on to the standing stones. Walking up to the entrance, I was disappointed to see that the café was closed!

"It's Sunday" Al grumbled, "everything is bloody closed on Sundays". It seems even pre-Christian sites aren't exempt from the rules of local religion. Doing washing on a Sunday is forbidden for the religious here. The Sabbath is strictly observed. Even going for a walk for pleasure used to be frowned upon.

We wandered around the stones in defiance of religion. Supposedly these are the most complete stone circle in Europe and were built somewhere between 2900-2600 BC. They are sited in a cruciform shape with the main circle of 13 stones in the centre. There's also a chambered tomb in the middle. This was built later than the initial stone circle.

It's been postulated that the stones are built to align with the moon as a kind of prehistoric lunar observatory. However, it's been pointed out that it also aligns, by chance, with a good deal of other events, making it impossible to say. It has also been rebuilt, and dug out of the 1.5 metres of peat which formed over the area, and so stones may well have moved.

The stones in legend are said to be petrified giants who refused to turn to Christianity and were solidified as punishment. Presumably this legend was created as a warning to wayward locals who were rejecting religion in favour of crazy ideas as being able to buy something to eat on a Sunday.

I walked around the stones for a while trying to take some nice photos. The view was pretty good from the hill.

Back at the visitor centre, we sat at a sheltered picnic table eating some of Al's chocolate. The guide book said there was a heathen shop which might be open on Great Bernera, an island connected to the west coast of Lewis by a bridge. It was about seventeen km away. If we left now we could possibly make it before it closed.

Al popped some more ibuprofen and we set off. The road wasn't easy, it weaved around and undulated as it made its way around the coast. Eventually we reached the connection to the island, Bernera Bridge, announced as being the first pre-stressed concrete bridge built in Europe.....bet they have to fight back the hordes of tourists. This bridge almost didn't exist. It was only constructed after the islanders, following a frustrating battle to get a link built, threatened to dynamite the nearby hillside to create a causeway!

We crossed and stopped for a moment to look at a couple of standing stones next to the road on the hill overlooking the bridge. While Al upended his bike to adjust his rear gears, I read a notice board providing some tourist information.

Great Bernera is roughly nine km long and three km wide and has a population of 250-ish. Nowadays its main industries are crofting, tourism and lobster fishing. It's famous as the site of the riots in 1874 when the locals rose up against the clearances by the landlord. For once the cause wasn't sheep, but the landlord wanting to expand his shooting estate which he called the 'Uig deer forest'. He even forced the locals to create boundary walls at their own expense. No wonder they were especially annoyed. Initially the bailiffs were fought off by the locals firing clods of earth at their heads, the crofters then took the fight in another direction by contacting a lawyer from Inverness, Charles Innes. The fight went to court and the crofters won. This event kick-started land reform across Scotland.

We cycled on for three km along the road which heads straight north up the middle of the island. Finally we saw a house with a small 'Post Office' sign hanging outside. It was open! We went in. "Hello" said a man who popped up comically from behind a counter. "You're open on a Sunday?" I somewhat redundantly said. "Yup, crazy huh?..........and everyone has to come to my shop!" he chuckled. We scoured the small but well stocked shop, and came back with enough to make a smoked sausage pasta meal, plenty of snacks, a bag of pears, breakfast, fruit cake, and some cans of coke to keep us going. "Where are you headed?" he asked, "Not sure, maybe we'll head back to Lewis and take the road to the west". There looked like there should be some nice beaches and coves. This was where the Lewis Chessmen were found. "There's a good spot on the north of Bernera" he said. "Follow the road up to Bostadh...there's a nice beach and iron age house." It sounded like a good place to stop for the night. It was also a shorter option, only five kilometres further, allowing aching knees a chance to recover.

We sat outside, opposite the shop, in a lay-by which overlooked a silvery lochan. Our seats looked like they at one time had been topped by petrol pumps. We refuelled anyway before setting off along the road.

Just to the east of us, away from any road is the site of a Victorian lobster pond. In the 1860s a large, stone wall was built across the opening of a small inlet. Lobsters and crabs were caught and kept fresh in the pond. In fact the pond environment was so agreeable to the lobsters that they started breeding to the surprise of the owner. This provided an easy source of product to be sold at market. In the 1950s the pond was used by the Crofters Supply Agency, who stored lobsters bought off of the local fishermen until the market price was favourable for selling on to France and Spain. In one year 28,000 lobsters were sold. Unfortunately, the pond is no longer used. Bet there's still some tasty lobsters still hanging about in there though!

We continued on up the empty single track road, the weight of our shopping slowing us down. A short ride later we reached the coast and the road turned before climbing extremely steeply. Al continued on up the hill, I made it about half way before getting off to push. The last few hundred metres was an easy roll into a small car park next to a cemetery. We explored the small beach and the high ground behind it and found a brilliant place to camp. After rolling our bikes across the bumpy hillside, we set up the tents in a sheltered area with a steep rocky cliff behind. Here we were well hidden from the road, and had an amazing view over the beach and sea below.

After setting out my sleeping bag to air and dry a bit, I climbed down to the beach for a walk. There was a small bird hopping about at the edge of the water looking for food. It may have been a dunlin. It ran along in front of me as I walked and didn't seem to concerned either with me or the small waves crashing over its head.

Further down the beach I came to a reconstruction of an iron-age house. In 1993 a massive storm hit this beach, revealing lots of very well preserved stone houses (fully excavated in 1996) which at one time probably covered the whole beach. These houses gave a wealth of information to the archaeologists, who guess that the village was occupied somewhere between 6-9 AD. They also discovered a Viking house which had been built on top of the earlier ruins.

The houses were re-covered with sand by the archaeologists to protect them, and a re-constructed house was built back from the beach, which is what I was now looking at. Unfortunately it was closed and locked so I couldn't see inside. I returned to the tents to start cooking up some dinner. It was a beautiful evening, and a beautiful place to camp. The man in the shop was right.

After eating, I lay inside the tent looking at the view and the wild flowers of the machair blowing in the wind.

Day 6

We again had a bit of a lie in. This was becoming a habit. It was 10 o'clock before I emerged from my tent and took in the view. I sat on the nearby rocks and ate some rolls for breakfast while waiting for the stove to boil some water for tea. The sun was shining and the sea was completely still, barely a ripple to be seen. I've had worse mornings. We were in no hurry to leave. I watched the world, oblivious to our presence, getting on with its day. The shimmering droplets of dew that had formed on my tent slowly rolled down and evaporated in the sun.

After a lazy start, it was time to head back down the road, past the post office/shop, across Great Bernera and then over the pre-stressed concrete bridge to Lewis. We were heading back down to Harris and towards the east coast town of Tarbert, but didn't really have much of a plan after that. We wanted to take it easy today to give sore knees and tired legs a chance to recover.

The guide book suggested that a road on the east side of the island was worth a visit. Called the 'golden road', the book told of remote single track road which passed around inlets and lochans. It sounded good. What sounded even better was a description of a shared bunkhouse "No 5, Drinishader" with sofas and a fireplace. We could do with a bit of comfort and a chance to dry out. Al phoned up and managed to book us into a room.

It was still a long way. At least the wind was behind us for a change.

We headed back down south on the main road. After passing the 'Welcome to Harris' signs, the hills once again loomed ahead. A long climb while dodging witless sheep later, and a short rest to recover, we hit the descent down to Tarbert. The speed and momentum of my heavily laden bike was scary. Without the weight I wouldn't have been concerned but as it was I looked at my bike

145

computer and saw that I'd reached the giddy new maximum speed for my trip of 45km/h. I chickened out of achieving anything greater and gently pulled on the brake levers.

We made it back down to Tarbert and decided to stop for some lunch. After looking around we settled on the 'Harris hotel' where we joined a few pensioners who were enjoying the warmth of the bar. I had a massive portion of fish and chips and a pint of ale. It was excellent.

With filled stomachs, and after having the forethought to visit a food shop for supplies, I struggled back onto my bike and we set of down the coastal 'Golden road'. It supposedly got its name from the high cost of building due to the difficult terrain. The road was built in the 1940s, after a long campaign by the locals, so that their kids could get to school. I imagine the children were delighted with their parents' tenaciousness!

The scene was one of grey rock everywhere, with small patches of green where some vegetation has somehow clung on or found a rare bit of earth to grow in. Although the road is never much more than a few metres above sea level, it feels like you are crossing the plateau of some great mountain as the road twists its way south. This rock is amongst the oldest exposed rock in the world, Gniess, formed over 3 billion years ago (or two thirds the age of the earth) and scoured smooth-ish by glaciers. The rock is pre-multi-celled life so doesn't contain any fossils. It so old that tectonic movements mean that it has travelled twice around the planet.

We stopped for a break and to take a look. I climbed a fence and jogged to the top of a small hill. From here I could see why people used the description 'miniature fjords'. The inlets may not have had the dramatic size of those I've seen in Norway, but they were certainly as picturesque. Little boats were attached to colourful pink buoys. The land looked like it was made of well-defined layers. A bright grey band of rock was sandwiched between the seaweed brown base and the grassy green layer on top.

We quickly covered the remaining seven kilometres to the bunkhouse and cycled up the drive for the earliest end to our cycling day for the whole trip. It was only 3pm as we checked in. I stood on the front balcony of the bunkhouse taking in the view for a moment. A giant, extremely fluffy ginger and white cat joined me. Clearly it liked the attention of all the visitors to the bunkhouse.

I hung my tent out on the balcony to dry and went inside for a shower before I offended the other bunk-housers with the smell of cycling.

With a fresh set of clothes on, we cooked up a great dinner of rice and more vegetables than I'd seen in a while, and made the most of the comfortable living room with its old leather sofas and fireplace. It's true that the long days of cycling meant I was sleeping well in a tent, but the first proper bed in a while did nothing to hinder matters.

Day 7

The next morning we enjoyed some coffee and a cooked breakfast while lingering in the comfort and dry until the early morning rain passed. Finally we headed off for our last full day on the Outer Hebrides. We were taking the ferry from Tarbert the following morning.

After reading in the guide about the possibility of seeing sea eagles, Al suggested we detour along the Huisinis road, a twenty kilometre long single-track road which runs out to the westernmost point of Harris. I agreed, and we set off along the not un-hilly road following along above the coastline. Down below I could see a large chimney on the shore and the remnants of some nearby buildings. The map marked this as "whaling station".

This was the Bunavoneader whaling station, set up by a Norwegian family who had the required shipping contacts. The chimney was to disperse the smoke, steam and fumes from the boiling apparatus used to clear the whale oil and fat. It was still running until the late fifties.

After processing, the products were taken by boat to Glasgow, the boats returning with coal and supplies for the whaling boats.

Lord Leverhulme bought the whaling station in 1920 (of course he did!). His plan supposedly involved using the whale fat to make soap. The meat, he would turn in sausages which he would sell in Africa. He also intended to dig a canal through the 'tarbert' to give easier access to the mainland for whaling transports. However, like most of his plans, this one never came to fruition, the canal was never built, and selling whale sausages in tins to Africans was surprisingly a failure.

We continued on along the road passing some hard surfaced tennis courts which stood out incongruously alone in the wild landscape.

The road dropped down, passing a waterfall, to the impressive building and manicured lawns of the otherwise uninteresting Amhuinnsuidhe Castle. Before passing right by the front door and heading back out into the rock filled heather. From here it became rougher, the tarmac embedded with rough stones which presumably are harder wearing, but slow cyclists down. The road rose up and past a couple of telephone masts, before dropping back down to the coast. Finally we reached the end and its sandy beach.

We cooked up some noodles at a picnic bench overlooking the quiet bay, before making the short trip along a sandy track to the other side of the headland. It was considerably windier around here so we didn't stick around for long.

The island of Scarp can be seen across the 500m sound. It was here that a crazed rocket scientist, Gerhard Zucker, attempted to improve the speed of mail delivery by experimenting with delivery by rocket. Unfortunately his first test of sending a letter failed. The postman brilliantly, and presumably glad that he wasn't about to lose his job carrying mail across to the island, collected up the remnants of the letter and marked it as "Damaged by explosion at Scarp, Harris" before delivering it by the usual method.

This being a dead end road, we turned around for the return trip. Just as we were at the highest point in the road Al shouted that he could see sea eagles. Sure enough, looking back there were three birds soaring above the coast which even from a distance looked huge. Al scrambled around in his pannier for a good few minutes before finally digging out some binoculars. We stayed and watched the sight of several of Britain's largest bird of prey with its distinctive white tail majestically soaring above the sea.

They eat a varied diet of pretty much anything they can get their talons on. They are so good at catching fish, that in the past Island fishermen thought the birds had supernatural powers which could be used to induce fish to surface and roll over ready to be caught. The fishermen also went to the effort of catching sea eagles and using their fat as bait in the hope of improving their catches.

Like almost every other bird of prey in Scotland, these were

149

persecuted by farmers, the last one being shot in 1918. They were reintroduced in 1985 and have been a bit of a success story, spreading along the west coast and islands.

As we set off again, the rain started. It was truly torrential. Even with what I thought was a decent waterproof jacket on, I was quickly soaked through. The steep inclines of the road surface weren't enough to stop large puddles forming.

We continued on back towards Tarbert. The ferry we planned to be on was due in the morning. We decided we just about had time to have a last detour. This time somewhere along the east coast, where we hoped to find a nice spot to stop for our last night on the Outer Hebrides.

Looking at the map, there was one obvious route out of Tarbert which we hadn't yet travelled. The road to the Isle of Scalpay. It was only about eight kilometres to the island, perfect. We were bound to find a nice spot to camp along the way, or maybe on the island itself, across the bridge.

We settled in for the, as always, undulating road. By the time we crossed the bridge it was beginning to darken. We needed to find somewhere quickly. However, it soon became apparent that the island, or at least the areas near to the only road, were quite well populated. This wasn't the sparse island I was expecting.

Scalpay had a single owner, Fred Taylor, until 2011, when he announced that he was handing it over to the islanders under a community ownership scheme. He inherited the island from his father, a wealthy architect. He did keep the tiny island of Scotsay as his permanent home though and built an eco, off-grid house there.

We cycled on, hoping for a break in the houses. We were running out of island when we came to a little car park at the end of the road. From here to the end of the island was empty heather. We pushed up a muddy path and soon found a decent spot where the tents were erected by torchlight. Our final night on the Outer Hebrides was spent cooking in the dark a lovely meal of vegetable curry. We headed off to bed as we'd have to wake early (by our lax standards) to make the ferry.

Day 8

We woke late. Packing things quickly, we didn't bother with breakfast. From where we were sitting, high up on the end of the island we could see the ferry coming in.....towards the slipway....which was a good 12km of undulating ride away. We sped back across the island, over the bridge and along the coast towards Tarbert. Somehow we made it in time, bought tickets and got onto the ferry for the 1.5 hour journey to the Inner Hebrides.

Skye

As we approached Uig, the remote ferry terminal at the western end of the Isle of Skye, the sky was looking ominously grey. We departed the boat and stopped off at "Uig Filling Station, Shop, Off Licence, Gifts, Groceries, Café and Takeaway" to restock with food. Rather than merely lacking focus, it seemed to be the only shop in town. After looking at the map, we decided to take the road down the west side of the island, which headed along the side of the excellently named Loch Snizort Beag. After this we took a turning at Skeabost and following the coast road around to Dunvegan. On the way we passed through the small village of Edinbane, founded by Kenneth MacLeod with money he'd made in India. When he was 15 he had travelled to India with a single golden guinea (a 2.5cm diameter coin of solid gold in his pocket which he'd been given by a neighbour. Originally worth one pound, although it quickly grew in value). He worked for a year before happening across the sale of a sugar factory, where he spent his Guinea on a large copper boiler. Taking the boiler to Calcutta he sold it for about 30 pounds, which he then used to return to the sugar factory and buy the whole remaining factory. He went on to use the factory to produce indigo dye (a distinctive blue organic dye extracted from plants) and made his fortune (because blue dyes were very rare) along the way.

Kenneth later returned to Skye and set up the village, ensuring that it had one craftsman for every required trade, and he also built up the first hospital on Skye.

Another first was electrical power. He built a lodge with it's own water turbine providing the first electrical lights on the island. The lodge was also used as a makeshift court, where the worst criminals were regularly sentenced to death, before being hung in the lodge gardens. Little wonder it's supposed to be haunted by several ghosts.

We continued on over the moorlands, on a road far more busy than we'd experienced on the outer islands, and down the hill into the town of Dunvegan. The Dunvegan Hotel looked inviting and we were hungry by now, so in we went. It was very quiet, empty but for us. There was a great view out the window of the curious flat topped mountains known as 'MacLeods Tables' across the water as we ate. The summits of these hills are almost exactly flat and level with one another. That level having once been part of a large flat plain. The mountains were formed by deep volcanic eruptions surfacing on the plain. Great glaciers later wore down the surrounding land leaving the harder volcanic rock lava spouts intact.

As always, there's a legend behind the formation of the mountains. It's said that St Columba visited the area but was refused any hospitality by the local Chief. Columba gave a sermon in a local church on a theme of rabbits having their warrens, birds having their nests, but himself, the messenger of the lord, having nowhere to sleep. At which moment, the ground shook violently, dark clouds filled the sky and there was a huge crash. On exiting the church the locals found that the tops of two nearby mountains had been sliced off, creating a bed and table for Columba to make his own.

We couldn't resist a coffee and cakes at a small shop on the way out of town. As we sat outside stuffing strawberry jam tarts into our faces we noticed a thatched building opposite which was called the 'Giant MacAskill museum'. Intrigued, once we were done at the café, I wandered over to take a look. It was open. I paid my two pounds and went in.

"Ahh....yer a cyclist" said the man inside noticing my clothes, "where are you from?"

I told him that I'm from Edinburgh.

"My sons a cyclist...he lives in Edinburgh, you might know him?"

"uhh...it's possible I suppose" I replied, not understanding where he was going with this.

"His name's Danny, he made some video on the internet that seems to be popular."

Click....my brain caught up. Of course...his son was Danny MacAskill, the trials bike stunt guy who become famous after a video of his amazing bike riding went viral. We chatted for a bit about the son he was clearly quite proud of. He showed me a wall covered in newspaper articles and pictures.

I turned my attention to the museum. It wasn't a giant museum at all, it was probably the smallest museum I've ever seen. In fact, it's dedicated to the story of the 'giant' Angus MacAskill who was about 8 feet tall and was born on the island of Bernaray in 1825. I learnt that he could apparently lift a full size horse over a fence, and that carrying 2 full size barrels packed with pork was no problem. What is true is that he moved to the US, where he is thought to have worked in a travelling show alongside Tom Thumb, the world's smallest fully grown man. He's in the Guinness book of records as the tallest true giant who ever lived, meaning that he didn't have any obvious medical conditions or deformities apart from his enormity. There were life size models of the pair in the corner of the room and a model of his giant chair that I sat in. All in all, I'd recommend a visit.

I returned to the bikes parked up outside. We took a look at the map and decided to head for the Sligachan camp-site, roughly in the middle of Skye and half way back to the mainland. We set off down the quiet side road along the west coast before heading inland with the amazing Cuillins rising up before us. These hills are arguably some of the most spectacular in Scotland. Mountaineers come from far and wide to tackle the jagged, raw mountain tops surrounded with deep gouged out corries and steep cliffs. Traversing the long ridges between the mountain tops in a single go has become one of the more difficult challenges people like to take on. These are called the black Cuillins simply due to the colour of the rock, which consists of gabbro, a very rough rock created when lava cooled.

We reached the Sligachan campsite late in the afternoon. Well known by outdoor types, this camp-site is right next to the main road across Skye as well as being the start point for many paths leading off into the bigger hills. Adding to the attractions is the hotel just across the road which provides a couple of decent bars and food for weary adventurers. Unfortunately, the camp-site also has one downside, and it's a big one. The surrounding boggy heather and sheltered cove provided the perfect habitat for one of Scotland's most ravenous creatures. Attacking on mass, they can't be scared off with noise or crowds of people. They can't be beaten back with weapons (excepting napalm or nuclear). No amount of fencing will hold them back. They are known as midge, and they are right little monsters!

As we found a suitable spot at the camp-site to erect our tents, we were quickly and quietly surrounded by tiny flies with hungry little mouths. Before I'd managed to get my tent out of my pannier I must have been bitten several hundred times. From experience, I find at moments like this the best way to deal with the situation is to swear profusely, run around so they don't have time to cluster around your body, and generally get whatever it is you need to get done finished before getting the hell out.

I pulled my cycling buff right over my face, and looking through the thin fabric, pulled a woolly hat out of my bag and jammed it on my head. My tent was up in record time, I threw everything inside and then dived in, quickly zipping up the door.

155

Squashing a few intruder midges against the top of the tent with a dirty t-shirt I lay back and breathed. Al was still out there, fighting.....I could hear him being even more angry than usual. I have experienced midges many times, (a particularly hellish time at the remote Corrour train station comes to mind) but I think the midges at Sligachan camp-site that day were the worst I've ever had to deal with.

One old guide book I'd read suggested dealing with midges by smoking a pipe, or that "standing next to someone who is being severely bitten can reduce your own attractiveness to the attacking midges. It is, however, unlikely the victim will remain standing still while being attacked". I prefer using Avon skin-so-soft, and so after retrieving a bottle from the bottom of my luggage, I applied it... liberally. It genuinely seems to work, although rather than repelling them it just kills them on contact with my now sticky skin. Meaning I end up wearing an attractive layer of dead flies. Still, can't complain.

We needed to eat so I ventured out once again to set the stove up and cook up some pasta. It was a nightmare. The sauce had a nice layer of midge on top. Half way through cooking a seagull appeared, and took a liking to the pan lid which it tried to escape with while I was being distracted by the flies. Al was laughing hysterically and, instead of helping, hid in his tent, peering out through the mesh door while offering helpful advice. We ate in my tent and after washing up made the decision to run for the pub. Later, unwilling to leave the comfort of the bar and having drunk more than we ought to have, we moved through to a smaller bar in the hotel itself where we ordered some whisky. We'd just settled down in the empty room when a rather posh gentleman arrived and sat in a nearby chair. He then droned on about how much 'Skye gets into your blood' and how he comes back every year to shoot things or something. We drank up and retreated to the preferable company of the midges and bed.

Day 9

The next morning was very grey, the midges were still about so we didn't hang around before packing while running in circles, and then heading off along the main road. The midges were certainly a good incentive to keep going at a certain minimum speed.

The route soon climbed up around the base of the black Cuillins. Just as we made it over the top of the hill the gentle rain which had started on the climb turned torrential. The road literally filled with water. Even with my full waterproofs on I was quickly soaked through. This being the main road, it was busy. Horrendously busy. Lorries passed too close, spraying up even more water. The lines of cars were never ending. I was still hungover. It was without doubt one of the most horrible cycling experiences I've ever endured. Skye was proving to be a massive disappointment. We reached Broadford and decided to take a break in the first café we could find. The lucky recipient of two dripping, soaking wet cyclists was the Beinn Na Caillich café.

We stripped off our sodden clothes and hung them up at the door. I emptied my shoes out and padded in soaking socks through the café, leaving wet footprints on the tiled floor. An hour later, substantially drier and full of tea and cake it was time to get going again. The rain hadn't stopped, which made leaving difficult.

The road continued in much the same manner for what seemed like hours, but eventually we reached the turn off. Instead of continuing along the main road and over the bridge to the mainland, we were heading to the south end of the island. Bridges are all good and well, and very efficient, but they aren't as exciting or interesting as a boat crossing.

Things off of the main drag improved significantly. The rain eased off, the traffic calmed, and even the tarmac was smooth and free from potholes. A big sign told us that the improvements were due to an EU funded road upgrade. Although it was still drizzling, I was no longer hating the ride quite so much. A substantial downhill roll for a few kilometres helped considerably.

We were now approaching the Sleat peninsula. Known as "the garden of Skye" due to its fertile soil and lush, heavily wooded hillsides.

We pushed on for 20km along the coast. Cycling alongside the rocky shore I spotted some movement by the water's edge. Stopping to take a look at first I couldn't see anything. I thought it must have been some seaweed moving in the water or something, but then I spotted a small furry body on a rock. It was an otter! It was snuffling it's way along the water front, oblivious to me standing not too far away. I watched for five minutes, before it slipped off into the water and around some rocks, out of sight. I think I've only seen otters in the wild maybe a couple of times. The memories of the crappy ride earlier in the day were already fading.

We reached Armadale and the ferry terminal. We had a quick look around, our ferry wasn't until the morning....the early morning! So we decided to continue along the coast on a smaller road and find somewhere to camp. On the way out of town we came across the Ardvasar hotel right next to the road. It has stood here since the early 1800s. It seemed rude not to have a visit and some ale.

We departed and headed along the road for the last night of our trip. Eventually we found a great spot right on a high spot above the coast, while hidden from the road. With the mainland and the magnificent mountains of Torridon visible in the distance. The tents were set up and after some dinner we decided to head back to the pub. Cycling without the weight of our luggage was once again a joy. Cycling back again after a few pints in the dark was also fun. I lay in my tent with the door open and looked out at the distant lights of Mallaig across the water as I fell asleep.

Day 10

We awoke in plenty time for once. After a leisurely breakfast we packed for the last time and headed back along to the ferry in Armadale. The trip across to Mallaig was too short. It was soon time to board the train and head back home.

West Coast Route:

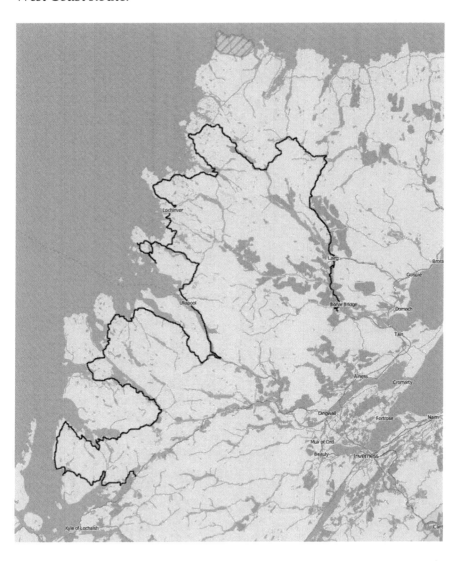

West Coast

We were on the move once again. Al was joining me once again for another week of exploring on bikes. This time we were headed to the west coast of Scotland. The almost mythically beautiful part of the mainland. Marked out by quiet single-track roads, a lack of people and wild scenes of majesty, this area has been the destination for more adventurous tourists since the middle of the 18th century when an admiration of order and harmony developed into a love for romanticism and hence, places of immense beauty. Previous concerns about visitor's personal security died along with the Jacobite cause, when stability arrived in the mountains. Partly this was also due to the lack of people on the land after the clearances. The wilderness became something to be enjoyed rather than feared. Soon, the growing English middle class at the start of the 19th century were afforded privileges previously only available to the aristocracy. They now had the time and money for their own expeditions. But rather than following the wealthy on grand tours of Europe, they preferred to head to remote areas of Britain that popular travel writers such as Wordsworth and Keats visited before them. People wanted something authentic, a real experience of something different.

We'd both visited various parts of the coast many times, but we'd never cycled the length of it.

The journey, even before the first pedal was turned, was long. I left my work in Edinburgh on a Friday night and drove across the busy M8 motorway to Al's flat in Glasgow. Here, I parked up outside, wondering slightly if parking near to a dodgy looking pub for a week was a good idea. I had a nice meal with Al and his girlfriend (now wife) and after perusing their bookcase I borrowed a book (Kerouac's 'On the Road') as I'd forgotten to pack one.

Stuff was messily transferred between cars and then we set off north in Al's Skoda. It was much nicer than my old car. Progress out of the city was slow. It was busy. The dual-carriageways were all restricted to 40 miles per hour. Though we didn't get close to going this speed. Eventually, we escaped the tight grip of the city. The roads widened and the cars thinned out. Soon we were passing Stirling and then making our way onto the main road north up the centre of Scotland, the A9. It was getting on, and even the late summer sun had set as we drove through the Cairngorm Mountains and listened to music. We were headed towards Al's mum's house in Speyside. As if to let us know we were getting close to the end of our road trip, and the area most synonymous with the national drink of Scotland, the last bit of the journey along small country roads was impeded by a slow moving whisky tanker.

Day 1

The following day started slowly and lazily with a lie in. I was tired after a busy week of work and the eventful evening before. I lay on my temporary bed, awake, watching, through a skylight, the clouds racing across the sky above me. I wondered what the next week held in store. Hearing some commotion in the kitchen downstairs, I dressed and made my way down, just in time for a large eggy breakfast with plenty of coffee. Plans were made, between mouthfuls of toast, for transport for the morning and soon we were stood on the drive outside the house transferring our belongings into another car. We were given a lift along the empty back country roads, at a speed and cornering confidence only a local could ever possess. We were taken, via a supermarket, to the nearby Elgin train station. Once again we transferred our gear, this time onto a train, for the hour's trip to Inverness where, after a late arrival, we rushed to make it onto our connecting train heading towards Kyle of Lochalsh.

While Al read a copy of the Economist, I passed the time examining the maps and watching the wild, tree and water filled landscape we were slowly passing through. Eventually, a couple of hours later, we broke out of the trees, passed along a wide and flat flood plain, and made it the remote station of Strathcarron. This tiny hamlet is situated at the head of the sea loch, Loch Carron and consists of a few houses, a post office and a hotel. It was also the start point of our trip up the west coast.

It rains a lot on the west coast. It was raining now. After watching the train depart we headed into the hotel for some shelter......and some beer. "No point in starting off the ride soaked!"

It was cold in the pub, but surprisingly busy. I guess this single pub services quite a large, remote, area and so has little other competition, the train station outside and road heading north bring in more customers.

After a time the rain eased off, turning from proper downpour to a light drizzle. Eager to get going, I put my waterproofs on before then putting some waterproof covers onto my pannier bags. We set out along the road before turning through the village of Lochcarron. The buildings here are strung out for a couple of kilometres along the shore of Loch Carron, partly a product of the clearances, it's coast-side location, unsuitable for sheep farming, meant that the people displaced were allowed to build homes along the shore. At the same time a new connecting road was completed allowing easy access to the town for folks looking for a new home.

We passed through, and continued on as the road headed up away from the loch, before passing through a gap in the hills. It was good to be finally going. I'd driven parts of the west coast before but never travelled the whole way. There's also something about seeing a landscape from a bike. You feel more connected, notice more, take in the smells and noises. The speed feels perfect. Unlike walking, you can cover big distances in a relatively short time, but you are still going slow enough that details aren't blurred.

As we rolled back down to the water at Loch Kishorn, I noticed an old man zipping along the road on a mobility scooter with a golf bag attached to the front, his long, grey beard streaming out behind in the wind. It was an arresting sight, out here.

The now quiet loch was once the site of a busy oil platform fabrication yard. The extremely deep water being suitable for such a task. In fact the world largest man made moveable object at the time, the Ninian Central platform, was built here in 1978. At 600,000 tonnes it must have been an impressive sight. Norway holds the current record with the 1.2 million tonne 'Troll-A' platform! Looking across to the north shore of the loch we could still see the huge, deep water, dry dock they blasted into the hillside to build the platform.

The fabrication yard had some interesting restrictions,

164

designed to protect the local environment. Supplies were only allowed to be delivered by sea, the 2000 workers had to live in temporary accommodation on the shore and on 2 ships (former passenger liners) moored in the bay. The restrictions worked. Once the fabrication yard wound down, the temporary buildings were removed and today little remains of the yard...... other than the giant hole blasted into the mountain!

Shortly past the village, we took a turn to the left along a side road. It was marked with a large blue sign which read "Road to Applecross, This road rises to a height of 2053 ft. with gradients of 1 in 5 and hairpin bends. NOT-ADVISED for learner drivers, very large vehicles or caravans after first mile". It didn't say anything about bikes. We stopped for a photo and then continued. This was the road up the Bealach-Na-Ba ("Pass of the cattle") which is one of the most dramatic roads in Britain. It's the closest thing we have to an alpine pass road, twisting its way over the mountains.

The first part of the road wasn't too strenuous. A gentle incline to start with as the view over the loch down to our left grew gradually more impressive. I was certainly warming up as I fought the pull of gravity. We turned a corner and worked our way up a steeper section of road. The vastness of the corrie the road was heading towards was now becoming clear. The huge, steep sided mountains looming up in front with the road heading right into the middle. Another long climb up and the road flattened out as it turned to follow the lip of the corrie. Ahh.......maybe the road wasn't going up this particular valley after all? Just as it looked like we were again turning north and along the inner edge of the hill, the road's path, hidden from view from us by the heather, turned sharply to the left and instead continued along the front of the mountains.

To our right now, above the rock strewn hillside, was the marshmallow shaped outline of Sgurr a Chaorachain at 792m. To out left was Loch Kishourn. We could now clearly see the deep water dry dock cut into the shore's edge right below us. A great solid looking, but presumably movable, barrier stretched across its wide opening. Looking further out to sea we could just about see Skye to the west and Plockton on the opposite shore.

On another holiday I took a boat trip from Plockton to see the seals and other wildlife in the bay. The owner of the boat, Calum, told me that he'd worked for years at the fabrication site, only making a career change when the place closed down. He seemed quite fond of previous job, although I'd imagine piloting a boat around these waters on a beautiful day is probably a damned sight better.

We turned another corner and the route of the road up the hill was now visible. This time I could clearly see that it headed directly into the heart of this hollow between the mountains, before rising steeply at the far end.

We pushed onwards. Once more it began to rain. I stopped for a few moments and donned my bright orange waterproof jacket. This jacket was probably more suited to city cycling. Al put on his more subtly coloured jacket.

Continuing on, the road again became steeper. It was also very narrow. In the BBC program 'Hamish Macbeth' they often filmed here. The sign seen in the show said simply 'Narrow road - no more than three sheep abreast'. We had to stop in the passing places to let a couple of cars past, but mostly, thankfully, the road was fairly quiet.

As we struggled upwards into the low clouds and viability deteriorated my legs were burning with the exertion. I was determined to make it to the top without stopping. The view back down the corrie as we made it to the hairpin switchbacks at the top was spectacular. I was wet, cold, tired and in some pain, but somehow I was enjoying the challenge. The road was now at its steepest, and at every hairpin the road reared upwards even more. I did my best to stick to the outside edge of the road around these corners, my pedal rate slowing almost to a stop even though I was in the biggest cog at the back and the smallest at the front. I was now sweating and roasting hot inside my jacket, but it was still raining so I didn't stop to take it off. Slowly nearing the lip of the hill, I pushed on, thinking about how the pain was about to end. I rounded a corner, passed a tiny lochan, and then raised my head from staring at the pedals to see the road climbing in front, once again. This time it really was the final long drag up. Ten minutes later I caught up with Al at a car park at the top.

From here the view is spectacular. Out to the west, the islands; Skye, Harris and Lewis in the Outer Hebrides, Rum and Rona, can be seen....on a clear day. Today, we could barely see the other end of the car park. We were shrouded in the low clouds moving in from the sea. After the self-generated warmth of the long climb it was now cold. The damp of my thin clothes providing little insulation.

We didn't hang about, it was time to go down the other side. We quickly dropped down the now smooth road. After a few minutes of rolling effortlessly, I was completely frozen. My hands were seizing up and becoming numb as the air rushed by. We wound our way past peaty bogs and watery heather, past rocks and reflective road side markers. Soon I caught up with a car, slowly making its way downwards. I had to slow, caught in the misty glow of brake lights. I urged it on, eager to reach the end of the road. Much as I'd looked forwards to the downhill while on the climb, now I realised it was actually worse. I had to stop for a couple of minutes in a pointless attempt to warm my hands by sticking them up my top. It also let the car get some distance. I set off again, now below the worst of the clouds. I could see the road stretching out over the moorland below and heading for the sea.

Soon after, we reached the end of the road in the coastal village of Applecross, or at least, the village everyone calls Applecross. Applecross is actually the collective name for all the settlements on this peninsula and estate. The main settlement we were now entering is marked as 'Shore Street' on maps. I'm going to go with popular opinion and call it Applecross anyway. Strangely, the estate itself is now owned by a charity, 'the Applecross Trust', none of the trustees of which, actually live in the area.

A visit to the village isn't complete without going to the 19th century Applecross Inn. It was past lunchtime and we were hungry and cold, so it sounded like the perfect place to stop. We leant our bikes outside a window of the whitewashed pub and found a table inside. This pub is famous for its fresh and decently priced seafood (the owner was even called Judith Fish!). Being hungry, both Al and I opted for haddock and chips. We drank hot tea and arranged our clothes on a nearby radiator as we waited.

Soon enough a waitress approached carrying a couple of heavily laden plates.....perfect! Al asked for some tomato sauce and as I got stuck in, he shook the bottle with a ferocity normally not reserved for condiments.

I heard a small scream, and looked up to see a girl, who'd been sitting some way behind Al holding her hands in the air. She had a light coloured dress on which had very recently had some additional colour applied to both it and her face. Others in the pub were also victims, although they looked less like someone had just attacked them with a knife. Other customers were by now either holding their hands over their mouths, or laughing. Al was looking at the now cap-less bottle of tomato sauce in disbelief. Clearly someone had not tightened the top. He stood up grabbed some napkins and started clearing the worst of the sauce off of the poor girl while apologising profusely. A waitress started cleaning the floor while others cleaned themselves. I sunk slightly down in my seat while laughing, trying to distance myself from the incident.

In the end, the girl didn't seem too upset. The pub got louder again as people relaxed. Al disappeared off to the toilet for some time to wash some relatively small stains from his top and then attempt to dry it using the hand drier. I ordered a beer.

Warmed and fed, we headed along the seafront road as it skirted Applecross bay. The weather had brightened while we in the pub. Once around the bay, the road continued to run along the shoreline, with the water lapping at the rocks just a few metres away. Across the water we could see the green, rounded hills of Raasay (home of the Raasay vole, a species found no-where else!), and the pointy dark black Cuillin mountains of Skye behind. A sailing boat was battling its way south, leaning over in the wind. We climbed a gentle hill before rounding a corner to see a sandy beach below. Huge dunes stretched up from sea level towards the road. I stopped and crossed some rough ground to the top of a dune and slid down.

With sand in my underpants, we rode on, past a waterfall by the road where we stopped to take a closer look at a large newt making its way thought the long grass. I've since looked at the photo I took and am pretty sure it was a great crested newt, the largest and rarest in the uk.

We were now adjacent to the island of Rona, or South Rona as it sometimes called to distinguish it from the other Rona to the north. As if to balance out Rassay to the south, this island is completely devoid of mice and voles.

The road headed away from the shore and passed through a few remote houses at Cuaig. Shortly after this we passed an isolated wooded building, not much larger than a shed. A sign announced it as 'The Weaving and Wool centre'.

Soon after we passed another tiny hamlet, Fearnmore. Here the road turned away from the open sea and along the southern edge of Loch Torridon. We decided to stop early and enjoy the scenery so as we cycled along we kept an eye out for a suitable camping spot. A contender was found just before Kenmore. A small hillock at the edge of the road looked promising. We jumped the fence and climbed over the hillock to find a good spot. It was hidden from the road but gave fantastic views of the loch. We dragged out bikes and luggage over the fence and soon our tents were up. Below was the tiny island of Eilean Mor, again confusing as there's another island called Eilean Mor on the other end of the peninsula.

We cooked up some food and sat inside my tent enjoying the shelter from the wind. We'd cycled sixty-five kilometres today. Not bad for a ride which had a very late start and a massive hill, while carrying all our camping gear.

Day 2

A gale was blowing. I was woken early by the noise of the fabric of my tent flapping around. To be fair we were in a very exposed position, with nothing to block the wind coming in off the open Atlantic. Looking out the door, without leaving the warmth of my sleeping bag, I could see the inlets up the loch sparkling in the low morning sun, the headlands between were dark silhouettes. The sky looked promising though, quite a lot of blue was showing between the clouds racing eastwards.

I heard some loud grumbling for the other tent,
"Al....Al..........Aaalll.......are you awake?".
"Yeeeessss" came the laboured and annoyed sounding reply.
"Time for breakfast?"
"I'm coming over"
Some scrambling noises later and Al dived through the door still inside his sleeping bag. We ate a cold breakfast with some hot tea and then packed up, tents flailing wildly in the wind as their supporting poles were removed.

The wind calmed as we made our way along the undulating coast road and into the village of Sheildaig. This community was established in 1800 with the aim of training and supplying seamen for the Napoleonic wars. The Navy offered grants for those interested to set up home here. After Napoleon's defeat and exile to Elba the grants stopped and the villagers turned to fishing. They were in an excellent spot for this as even the Vikings had been impressed by the vast amounts of herring found in the nearby waters.

We trundled along the seafront road lined by whitewashed houses. This was certainly a picturesque place. Al stopped at a picnic table to check a problem he was having with his rear wheel. I joined him. He set about investigating a soft, but not flat, rear tyre.

Just off of the shore is an island which was, in contrast to the hills surrounding the village, covered in tall straight trees. Now owned by the National Trust, the trees were planted to, depending on what you read, provide masts, poles for drying fishing nets or timber for the navy. I was distracted by the thwack, thwack, thwack of Al furiously pumping up his tyre. No idea why it had gone flat, it seemed to be holding up now. So we set off again.

Soon, the mighty mountains of Torridon, all of which are Munros, appeared across the loch we were following; Upper Loch Torridon. The tell-tale metal rings of fish farms could be see packed closely together on the water, the clear waters perfect for producing salmon and mussels.

As we rounded the end of the loch, the layers of rock which made up the mountains could clearly be seen. Unimaginable forces and time have colluded to build these mountains. The bottom layers are made of rock which is three billion years old and two thirds of the age of the planet, Lewisian gneiss. This was formed as the hot, liquid mantle of the earth first began to cool, hence it contains no fossils. Above this are layers of only slightly less old sandstone and this is topped by the white of Cambrian quartzite. Some of the best mountain bike routes in the country run through these mountains. The sandstone providing a nice grippy surface for riding on.

We'd only cycled a scant twenty-six kilometres, but on reaching 'The Torridon Inn' we decided to have an early lunch. An internet connection inside provided an opportunity to email back home, data phone signals being a rare breed up here.

Refreshed, we headed along Glen Torridon, the road followed a river along the base of Liathach. Many climbers and walkers rate Liathach as Scotland's finest mountain. The route along the ridge being a challenge even for the experienced.

It was just adjacent to this mountain where an aviation disaster prompted the formation of the Mountain Rescue services. In 1951 a Lancaster bomber, which had been converted for reconnaissance missions, was flying from RAF Kinloss in Moray, to an exercise near Rockall, way out in the Atlantic Ocean. On its return in terrible weather it crashed into the top of Beinn Eighe, just 4-5 metres below the summit! For two days the crash site was unknown until a boy, when he heard about the missing plane, reported that he'd see a red glow from the mountain.

The RAF had located the plane, but for several days couldn't access the site due to bad weather. The RAF teams weren't trained or equipped for such terrain and they initially refused help from local mountaineers. Eventually they made it, and recovered a body. It was almost six months later that the final bodies were recovered. Following this, the first Mountain Rescue team was created.

I've walked up and into the corrie where the crash happened. There's a small loch which a stream leads from, dropping off the lip of the corrie like an infinity pool. At the other end of the loch is the massive triple buttress. Three adjacent cliffs, the top of which the plane crashed into. Even now, sixty-five years later, wreckage is strewn around the spectacular corrie.

The next twelve kilometres was an easy ride into Kinlochewe, where we joined the main road to the north. We started to climb along the edge of another loch. This time the twenty kilometre long 'Loch Maree'. In the past, being dunked in the waters of the loch was thought to a cure for lunacy. The irony of the act obviously bypassing the participants.

The loch has a couple of other claims to fame, the first being that it contains the only island, which has its own loch, that in turn contains an island. The other is that it has its own monster, the 'Muc-sheilche' (loosely translates as 'turtle-pig') which lived here, but travelled to other lochs in the area. Around 1840, the locals prompted the estate manager, Mr Bankes, to try and find the monster by attempting to drain the nearby 'Loch-na-Beiste' in which the 'beiste' had been spotted on several occasions. At first they ran a literal two-horse power pump for the best part of two years, but to little effect. The level of the loch just sank by a few inches. Next, he tried to poison it with fourteen barrels of lime, presumably hoping the monster would be killed and float to the surface. However the monster stayed undiscovered. Perhaps he was just off visiting another loch at the time?

We stopped for a while at a viewpoint and took in the view. The sun was out and though there was still a slight wind, it was warm...which made a nice change. The view was dominated by the mountain of Slioch on the opposite side. This must be one of the most familiar mountains of Scotland. No calendar being complete without a photo.

Cycling onwards along the A832 was quite different to what had come before. The next sections of road were defined by gentle long straight climbs. It wasn't too busy either. It didn't take us long to cover the next twenty kilometres. The road changed back to single-track as it passed through a tight valley and along the side of another loch. We stopped at a green tin hut next to a small car park. This was where the main path into the Loch Bad na Sgalag native pine-wood begins. This is a protected area of a newly re-introduced pine species which grew here before it was all cut down to produce charcoal. A walker approached and launched into what sounded like a well-rehearsed talk about the area. I think he was involved in the replanting. When he'd finished his short presentation, we told him about our route and he mentioned a restaurant not far away. It was a small detour off of the road we were taking, but worth it, he suggested.

It sounded good, so when we reached the turn-off a few kilometres further on, we took it. The road wiggled its way four kilometres to the small shore-side settlement of Badachro. As we made our way down a tiny side road towards the sea, we emerged at the front with a beautiful natural harbour in front of us. There were several boats in the harbour including a small fishing boat. Further out in the water, protected from the open sea by an island, sat a few sailing boats. Walking out to the end of a stone jetty I could see a colourful mess of small boats and canoes pulled up onto the grassy banks further around the bay. We easily found the pub the walker had mentioned, ' The Badachro Inn' and went in.

Looking at the selection of ales on offer, my attention was caught by one called 'Bealach na Ba', having crossed the pass the day before, I couldn't have chosen anything else. We sat at a table overlooking the sea. It was stunning place. The clear water of the cove sparking in the sun, with deep greens and blues emanating from the shallows.

Our plates of seafood soon arrived and we snaffled it down. Delicious...and not too expensive either.

I wondered about going further along the dead-end road to find some place to camp for the night, but Al was keen on heading further north up the coast to see how far we could get in our week. Fair enough. Full of energy, we returned back to the main road and took a left.

A few kilometres later, we passed through the quiet village of Charlestown shortly before arriving at Gairloch. There are a few settlements close together that are collectively known as Gairloch. This is a result of the local landowners and clan leaders, the Mackenzies, refusing to evict tenants during the clearances, to their own detriment. In fact people evicted from elsewhere were welcomed here.

By now it was beginning to get late, and had almost reached the point where lights would be needed. I dug out and switched on my back light as we continued up the road looking for a place to stop for the night. Four kilometres further on we found a great spot next to Loch Tollaidh. Exploring down a small track leading to the loch-side we discovered a flattish small peninsula sticking out into the loch....perfect.

As the sky darkened, a few midges were flying about, but nothing too bad. I walked about in the heather looking for the best place to sleep. I heaved a rock off of the flattest tent sized area and set about constructing my home for the night. For once, the view was nice, but not spectacular. I could see some hills in the distance to the north, but the view was predominantly of heathery plateau. We settled in, glad to have stopped for the night. We'd only cycled eighty-eight kilometres, but the hills and undulating roads had made it feel like much further. After eating a big meal. We sat chatting by the loch side, watching the lights of the very few cars heading along the road. The occasional plop of fish could be heard as they started to rise, jumping out of the water feasting on the flies now hovering above the shimmering surface.

Day 3

After a late start, we rolled the couple of kilometres from our camp site and into the town of Poolewe. We had a quick look around the tiny settlement and stopped to buy some supplies in the small shop. We had planned to just eat breakfast from the shop, but on finding a nice looking coffee shop we decided to go in. A quick look at the menu showed a surprising diverse range of options for a tiny coffee shop. I had some salmon on some nice toast.

Fed and caffeinated, we hit the road, keen to get some kilometres behind us. We shortly passed Inverewe botanical gardens. The climate here, powered by the Gulf Stream, provides a warmth that allows plants to flourish that grow nowhere else at this northerly latitude.

Later, looking out into Loch Ewe, we could see the Isle of Ewe. Due to the name which sounds like 'I love you', it has now become popular for couples to take a boat trip around the island.

The road was good, and we soon passed Aultbea and climbed the hill to the other side. We sped down the far side and past Laide. We rode on for 5km along the edge of Gruinard bay and through the villages of First Coast and Second Coast. The nearby island we could see, 'Gruinard Island', is the former site of biological warfare testing by the military. In 1942 a highly virulent anthrax bomb was developed and then deployed here against some test sheep. The bombs were fixed to the ground before being detonated. The sheep died days several days later. The tests were deemed a success and the impossible task of decontaminating the islands immediately after the tests was used as further proof that it would be an effective weapon against Germany, rendering large urban areas inhabitable for long periods of time. In fact the island wasn't successfully cleaned up until 1990, after a long campaign including a group called 'Operation Dark Harvest' who reportedly collected samples of soil from the island and sent it politicians and the military research facility which developed the weapon. The experiment has since been declassified and there's some pretty interesting and comprehensive film of the experiments available on the internet.

Foregoing a nice island boat trip, we continued on and came to a long steep hill. At the top of the long slog a lay-by provided an opportunity for a rest and a view of Gruinard Bay directly in front with its sandy beach.

Beyond the beach we overcame another big hill. Then came an easy and relatively uneventful ride through the relatively treeless but mountainous area marked as 'Dundonnell Forest' on the map. Presumably another casualty of former tree clearing and contemporary sporting estates. We already had fifty-five kilometres behind us as we rolled down to the Falls of Measach at Corrieshalloch Gorge.

The road thus far had been very pleasant to cycle on, quiet, relaxing, with time to admire the views rather than concentrating on avoiding traffic. This changed abruptly when we turned onto the main road to Ullapool. It was a long slog which we just had to get on with. We had no route choice, this is the only road that connects to the north from here. The road was busy and the traffic was moving too fast with little regard for how close they were passing. Sometimes the road would be straight, there'd be nothing coming in the opposite direction but still cars would pass with only inches to spare. The lorries were actually better, at least they pulled out a bit to get past.

The road seemed longer than it had looked on the map. Ten kilometres along it we stopped for some relief at a parking area overlooking Loch Broom. Al sat on the warm tarmac with his back to the water, saying his knees were hurting again. We'd been pushing it hard along the road, eager to get somewhere more pleasant. We sat in silence for a while. Looking at the map I figured that we had about another ten kilometres to go to reach Ullapool.

We moved on along the torturous road and eventually made it into the outskirts of the small but busy town. I stopped for a few minutes at the shore side to take a few photos of scenery complete with the big Cal-Mac ferry which was just leaving, heading for Stornoway in the Western Isles some fifty miles away. People were out on the deck watching the view as they slowly slipped away. I couldn't help but wonder about who the majority of the people were, tourists, or people who lived out there?

We continued onto the main street of the town and found a spot to stop and contemplate our next move. It was now the late afternoon and we didn't have a plan of where to stop for the night. Not that we'd worried about that at any time before. However, on spotting a proper camp-site on the map, four kilometres up the coast, we thought it'd be a good option. It'd be great to have a shower at any rate. The camp-site looked like it was in a nice spot, sticking out into the water on a small peninsula.

Now we had a plan, we had some time. We enjoyed some fish and chips in a nice pub on the front.

At the camp-site we found a quiet spot at the side and unpacked. After hanging some damp clothes on a guy rope to dry in the sun I noticed our neighbours had a bright orange tandem mountain bike. I went over to chat to them.

After discussing our relative trips and where we'd been. He asked if we'd like a go on the bike. Of course! We jumped at the chance. The guy sensibly stayed at the front controlling things while we each had a go at the back, riding around the road circling the interior of the camp-site. It was slightly odd to be on a bike without having turn-able handlebars. Even starting off you normally turn the handlebars to counteract any overbalancing. Somehow it works the rider on the front just does this job for two. We cycled slowly around the track and then over the grass up a small hill, the long wheelbase on the bike not making any discernible difference to going off-road. I can see the appeal, no-one ever falls behind and the effort is shared when going up hills or when tired. However, I'm not sure of the attraction of sitting looking at someone else's back, or not

178

being able to just ride along on your own for a while. Still, others seem to enjoy it. I once saw a couple ride over a giant bike see-saw at a trail centre on one, they made it look easy.

I also took part in a OMM Bike (Original Mountain Marathon) race in Yorkshire against a couple on a tandem. I think they came in the top 10 despite the rough terrain, proving that they certainly aren't a hindrance.

It was a lovely night. Before bed, I went for a walk along the pebble beach next to the camp-site and watched the orange glow of the sun as it disappeared between the mountains. Some children were skimming stones across the water, breaking the silence with happy noises.

On the way back to my tent, I noticed some people were camping out in what looked like a massive military truck, complete with huge knobbly wheels. I wondered where the truck had been before it's conversion to a family camper. There was no-one about to ask.

Day 4

We were off again. We started up the curiously named Glutton pass. The road north of Ullapool was much quieter and again cycling along was a pleasant experience as we climbed a ponderous hill before rolling down the far side and through the small croft of Strathcanaird. Soon we came to a turning where we took a left on a tiny road signposted 'Lochinver' and entered the 'North West Highlands Geopark'. This is an area encompassing sites of scientific importance and is properly defined as 'an area which advances the protection and use of geological heritage in a sustainable way, and promotes the economic well-being of the people who live there'. They are very much tied in with tourism, both promoting interesting geological features, and local heritage. Translated into normal language, there's some cool stuff to see nearby.

We headed down the new road, now travelling directly west. The massive mountains reared up on our right hand side. Soon we turned a corner and the vista opened out. I spied the distinct shape of Stac Pollaidh in front with its steep sides and rocky pinnacled 'hat' on top. Apparently it's not too difficult to climb despite its foreboding appearance.

We pootled along the road for another ten kilometres or so. The ancient rock providing such magnificent views, prompted me into thinking about the age of the planet. The ice age which sculpted these rocks only receded 14,000 years ago. The tiniest fraction of Earth's history. We think of our home as stable, human friendly environment. Instead it's in a constant state of flux, entirely indifferent to our short existence. It owes us nothing.

The road turned northwards around the base of the mountain. We decided to spend a bit more time in this area and instead took a turn-off which headed south towards the coast. A little way along and I was surprised by the strange flatness of the area around the small Loch Osgaig. In contrast to the steep stony hillsides we had just past this area looked like it had been levelled by bulldozers before someone had layed a uniform carpet of brown heather down on top. We cycled along the Sceletrix track of a road which had been built on top of the carpet. Luckily neither of us were flung off the track when negotiating the corners.

Coming down to the coast we were rewarded with a fantastic view of the dark, ominous looking Summer Isles. They may have been an inspiration for the fictional 'Summerisle' in the horror film, 'The Wicker Man' although it was all filmed much further south in Dumfries and Galloway. Some old ladies in head scarves were standing looking at an information board and as I approached they turned and one gave a little scream of alarm. I wasn't aware that I looked quite that scary. I tried a friendly "Hello!" They mumbled something back before scuttling off towards a parked car. The woman from the shop from the weird and dark comedy series 'League of Gentlemen' came to mind. Odd. I read the sign and took a few photos as the car crawled past and turned back up the hill.

The road turned to follow the scattered houses along the shoreline. We cycled through Polbain. It must be amazing to live here in these houses with amazing views. In places such as this I always wonder, what do the people do? How do they manage to live and work in such a remote place? More importantly, how can I do the same? What do I have to do?

We came to Polbain stores. A small whitewashed shop with a red tin roof and simple painted sign hanging over the small doorway. Al went in to buy something while I waited outside. There were chickens wandering about in the road. I walked up and took some photos. They watched me with their beady little eyes and made small noises.

A couple of kilometres further along the coast and we arrived in Achiltibuie. The name translates from the Gaelic as 'Field of the yellow-haired boy'. Presumably blond haired kids were rare at the time when it was named. We passed a modest pebble-dashed house which had a large helicopter landing pad out the front. There was a sign on the fence which said '3 Dolphins Bed & Breakfast'. At first I thought it must have been an attempt at attracting the jet-set to stay, but apparently the owner just applied for a license and then built the helipad with her own money to allow rescue helicopters access to the area for the benefit of the local community. Pretty nice thing to do!

Further down the road we came to the Achhiltibuie gardens. They are set in the former site of a hydroponicum, where fresh fruit and vegetables, including bananas, were grown indoors all year around for use by the nearby Summer Isles hotel (the previous former film-director owner of which, started the project) and for selling to the locals. The project also attracted up to 10,000 visitors a year before it was sold.

We stopped at the hotel for a drink and sat in the sun in the garden, watching a curious mixture of fully leather wearing motor bikers sitting drinking soft drinks on a wall and posh people wearing garish but formal, striped shirts and driving huge SUVs eating massive plates of food at the tables. Two men at the next table were loudly discussing their next choice of car. Too loudly...we got up and moved to sit on the grass.

I was enjoying this day the most out of the journey so far. We'd cycled a not too bad fifty kilometres already and still had plenty more hours of possible cycling. The sun was out warming the air and we were sitting drinking beer overlooking the island of Tanera Mor. Things were pretty good.

Tanara Mor is the largest of the Summer Isles, it now uninhabited. In case you fancy living there and have some spare change, the owners are currently trying to sell it for a bargain price of £2 million.

We headed back up the road and took a short cut back to where we rejoined the Scaletrix track again. The mountain scene ahead of us showed an interesting thing in that all the flat tops were in line at the same level. Showing the original ground level before the ground rose up as the ice receded and the bits in-between were worn away. This time we continued north and worked our way through some lovely wooded countryside. Quite different to the heather. For the first time, there were small birds flitting about.

As we reached the small settlement of Inverkirkaig, the view opened up and Suilven with its saw toothed top could be seen in front of us. For once this mountain isn't named in Gaelic, but in Viking Norse. It translates roughly as 'pillar mountain'. This area and the village were settled by Vikings. Before that, when the ice was hundreds of metres thick, the top of Suilven was a 'nunatak', a term new to me, it means an island of rock sticking out above the glacier wearing it's sides away as it squeezed past.

We continued on for another three kilometres where we reached the town of Lochinver, the second largest fishing port in Scotland and the one where most of the European fleet scouring the seas to the west, come to offload and sell their catches. It's not the most beautiful town. There wasn't anything here for us, so we moved on to begin our daily hunt for a camping spot. "Somewhere with a view!" I'd say. "What is it about you and 'having a view'?" Al would reply. A vaild question. Mostly you're just inside your tent. Invariably, spots with a view were also exposed spots and so windier and colder. However, the argument for having a view is all about waking up, opening the door of the tent and while still snuggled up in a comfy sleeping bag, and watching the world for that short period before it's time to get up. Otherwise what's the point of all this? I'm not cycling to not enjoy the scenery.

We cycled on for another eight kilometres before, just when the sky was beginning to darken, we finally found a spot. There were some scattered houses not too far away, but to go on and try and find somewhere more remote would have been pushing things. I checked my bike computer, we'd cycled just over 100km. We were happy to stop. The raised hill even had a view! And we found some shelter from the wind next to a small knoll. A nearby rock provided us with a table of sorts and we had quite a civilised meal which we followed up with the remnants of some uisce beatha which translates as 'water of life', and was the name the ancient Celts gave to the fiery alcohol now known as whisky. Hip flask emptied, and the chat being replaced by the sound of the cold wind, we headed for bed.

Day 5

The next day I awoke to the patter of rain on the tent. I lay in the warmth, my blow-up, fleece covered pillow squeaking as I shuffled around to get comfortable. After a few minutes of procrastinating I unzipped the door and peered out into the cold air. The rain wasn't as bad as it sounded. It was actually quite a bright looking day. After some breakfast and coffee, we packed up the tents and gear, rolled our bikes back down to the road and set off once again. This time wrapped up warm in extra layers and waterproofs.

Soon, we were warming up, cycling up and over the undulating hills. Passing a wood, we stopped to take a look at some large grey game birds with white heads which were hanging about in the long grass at the edge of the road. I'm not entirely sure what they were. They looked like partridges only larger.

Around the corner we arrived at Drumbeg, set in beautiful surroundings. The main part of the strung out settlement looked out over Loch Dhrombaig, not really a loch, but a bay protected from the open sea by a cluster of small islands.

We stopped at the heavily signposted Drumbeg stores. I went in to find not only the usual essentials, but an unexpectedly vast choice of local products to rival any deli in Edinburgh. Sitting below the baskets of fresh bread and cakes, the smoked fish looked particularly good. The shop also sold a large selection of good beer, wine and whisky. We stocked up.

A couple of kilometres later we passed through "Nedd". It was here, in 1830, that a travelling pedlar was murdered. Murdoch Grant had been in the area to attend a wedding. Several weeks later he was found floating face-down in nearby loch with his pockets emptied of the considerable amount of cash he was believed to have been carrying. On being dragged from the loch it was clear an act of violence had befallen him. For some time the local policeman, Mr

Lumsden, investigated but failed to uncover any clues. He was given some assistance in his investigations by a local man Hugh MacLeod who was currently unemployed, possibly looking for something to engage his time, and living back with his parents after previously failing to set up a local school.

Later suspicion fell on Hugh MacLeod after he changed an unusually large denomination note at the local post office. Despite the weakness of this evidence, Hugh was arrested. His home was searched, but nothing was found, and so he was to be released. However, a tailor's assistant, Kenneth Fraser, appeared on the scene and claimed to have had a dream in which he was told of the location of the pedlar's pack; in a cairn of stones, close to Hugh's house, in a hole. When the police and Kenneth went to the location from the dream, they found some of dead man's possessions. Quite why Kenneth seemed immune to suspicion after doing this is anyone's guess. What did happen next is that somehow, despite the earlier searching of his house, Hugh MacLeod was now found to be in the possession of some of the pedlar's stockings. He was taken to Inverness where he was tried in court. Kenneth gave a statement on his dream as evidence and Hugh was sentenced to death, apparently confessing to the murder just before his sentence was carried out! The whole story is just odd.

We cycled on and over the very steep sections of road as it worked its way across the Assynt peninsula. The mountain range of Quinag was somewhere close by to the south-east but we couldn't see it or its massive buttresses from the road.

The range has some remnants of ancient woodland hanging on. In a positive move, the estate is now owned by the John Muir Trust who are working to restore and protect the local environment.

For the next seven kilometres the road undulated its way through the deep gulleys at the base of Quinag. We'd be braking as hard as we could going down a long steep hill, before letting go, and then pedalling like crazy to get some momentum up before climbing the steep hill on the opposite side. We stopped for some lunch at a nice point at the top of a downhill section overlooking the road on the other-side impressively zig-zagging its way up again.

The sun was out once more. I lay in the grass dozing and listening as Al filled an Italian moka pot with water and coffee before noisily screwing it together and precariously balancing it on top of his stove. A lighter clicked a few times before the gas lit with a whoosh. As the water in the pot slowly heated and reached boiling point, it turned into steam in the lower chamber. The expanding gas forced the remaining hot water up the central pipe where it soaked through the coffee grounds at about 90degrees C, apparently the perfect temperature. Continuing its way up, the water, now coffee, quietly hissed as it flowed out into the upper collection chamber. Steam and coffee smell rose out from the small spout. Finally as the water ran out, the characteristic gurgling noise of the moka pot grew louder indicating that it was ready. Al poured it out and handed me my beaten up, old plastic mug.

Re-energised, we made our way over the remaining hills until the road flattened out and the small back road we'd been following rejoined the main road north. A fast and long downhill took us the couple of kilometres to the village of Kylesku. Until as late as 1984 this used to be a dreaded bottleneck on the way north as a small ferry was the only way to continue. Today we'd be crossing the bridge. Before this though, we made a small detour down the waterfront where we found a nice pub in the Kylesku Hotel. Sitting outside the front at a table, we watched as about ten people advised a man on the best way to get his small dinghy, which was currently on a trailer attached to a four by four, down a boat ramp and into the water. A lot of pointing and gesturing was taking place. In the end, the man reversed, steered the side of the vehicle into some metal barriers, drove forwards again, before reversing once more, but this time too far into the water. Apart from the difficulty in getting out of the massive car when it was sitting in several feet of water, it looked like maybe he should have untied the boat from the trailer before putting it into the water. The boat was floating, but so was the trailer, still attached to the bottom. A small crowd was now gathering to watch. The man was getting angry. More people were now sticking their oar in……

As the drama continued, I read a brochure about local boat trips up the loch to Eas a' chual Aluinn, Britain's highest waterfall, or rather, the waterfall with the largest drop from top to bottom. The distance being about 200 metres.

The sea lochs, 'Glencoul' and 'Gleann Dubh', which meet where the bridge crosses, were the testing and training sites for X-craft midget submarines during the Second World War. These were designed to be towed by normal full-sized submarines before being released near to their intended areas of operation. Crew could be shuttled between the main and midget submarines using a dinghy. The craft were specifically designed to attack the German fleet while in Norwegian Fjords. The size of the craft would enable the quiet placement of explosives which would be detonated by timers on the shallow sea floor underneath enemy vessels. They were powered by the same diesel engine as used on London buses, as well as a much quieter electric motor for use when close to the enemy. An airlock was added to later submarines to allow a diver to exit and place charges. In the end, they took part in multiple missions but weren't hugely successful, although they did do extensive damage to the huge ship Tirpitz, sister ship of the Bismarck. However, they were used extensively for surveying and other preparation work for missions using other equipment.

In time, we left both the hotel and the man who was still struggling with his boat on the slipway. As I reached the junction back at the main road, I looked to the right to check no cars were coming, then I looked left, to see a massive stag standing looking at me from about ten feet away! He stared for a few seconds as I panicked and almost fell off my bike. Then he turned his head and started munching on a bush at the side of the road.

I dragged my bike away to the other side of the road and then took a few photos, before jumping back on and chasing after Al, who had by now disappeared down the road. I caught up on the other side of the bridge where he'd stopped in a lay-by and was reading a sign on a small memorial cairn erected to commemorate the 50th anniversary of the x-craft submarine missions. It read: "The security of these top secret operations was guarded by the local people of this district who knew so much and talked so little".

A long hill took us up and through Duartmore Forest and past the very scenic Loch Duartmore, surrounded by purple heather. Again we climbed, this time me in front for a change. I stopped at a lay-by. Al caught up and came to a stop with a grimace. "Dave, remember last trip. Well, I think my knee is bollocked again!"...It was time to get the ibuprofen out.

There were some ludicrously long straight sections of road over the next ten kilometres. At least the cars could see oncoming traffic as they floored it past after miles of frustrating winding road.

We arrived in Scourie, passing the pretty hamlet of Badcall, we didn't stop there which was maybe a.......never mind. Scourie is set at the head of a rocky bay. There wasn't much to the place. The view out to sea was great which is probably why a busy camper van and caravan site was blocking most of the view of it from the road. I went into the small Spar shop. On paying, the girl behind the counter started asking about our trip. I recounted our journey so far as she stared at me with an uncomfortable intensity. Then she said "you have amazing eyes!". I felt myself turning red and mumbled something about "umm...thanks". I paid up and said something eloquent like "well....bye" before escaping out the door.

Outside, I told Al of my weird encounter. I don't think he believed me.

It was early afternoon and we needed to make a decision. We were running out of time on our week long trip. It was clear from looking at a map that, although we could have continued up to the north coast, from there we'd have quite a distance to get back to anywhere with a train station. For a moment we entertained the idea of detouring to try and make a visit to the nature reserve of Handa Island which was off the coast nearby. Originally used as a burial place as it was free from wolves which would dig up the graves, it had a small population until 1848, when the potato famine hit and forced the residents to emigrate. It's now known for the diverse range of birds which can be seen there and is a popular visitor attraction.

Instead, we'd now almost reached the last junction where we could take a road to the east. In fact the road headed south-east, all the way to Lairg which handily the train passes through. Taking this road we'd be able to get a train tomorrow. Leaving a day in hand so we could take our time to get back south and back to work.

We pedalled on another eight kilometres, enjoying momentary views of the sea as it appeared between scenic outcrops. This section of road is known as 'destitution road'. It was built to provide employment for people who were otherwise suffering due to the potato famine. The pay was pretty bad, often just oatmeal. But it was better than starving.

We finally said goodbye to the sea at Laxford Bridge, where we took the small single-track road to the east. The road was lined with old trees and followed a river for the next five kilometres before passing along the edge of a couple of lochs. It felt very remote. Most of the settlements in this area, Sutherland, are on the coast. There isn't too much inland. A few scattered houses and farms. The hills were now becoming more grass than heather, a welcome change in colour. Twenty kilometres passed quickly. Looking at the map during a break in cycling, it was clear we'd be in Lairg in a couple of hours...or...there was a tempting track road heading north, through the hills, for twelve kilometres. The far end of the track connected with a road that ran east and then south making a big loop which looked far more fun that continuing on our current road.

Of course we took the track. We headed up what we thought was the correct hill and cycled into a work site busy with fluorescent jacketed workers, 4x4s large trucks, and cables strewn across the large area which had been bulldozed obliterating the original path of the road. People stared as we made our way

190

through the muddy and deeply rutted area towards where it looked like the track continued. A man by the road asked if we were alright, while simultaneously giving the impression that we shouldn't be there. "Are we ok to go up this road?" I asked. "Yeah, no bother! Up there." he pointed. And so, on we went.

The track climbed steeply and after a while I looked back to see Al falling behind. This time it was on account of his thin tyres struggling with the road surface rather than knee issues. My tyres were also slicks, free from grippy knobbles, but they were much wider and were coping not too badly with the rough rocky surface. It was certainly a change from tarmac where you could more or less let your mind wander as you roll along. On rougher stuff, at least some brain capacity has to be dedicated to studying the terrain right in front and steering the path of least resistance avoiding rocks and muddy patches and the like. I like the sort of half meditative state this can sometimes induce where you are really thinking of nothing at all, the road is distracting you just enough to dispel usual thoughts. Suddenly, I'll 'wake' from this state and realise I've really no idea of the details of the last few kilometres where my sub-conscious has been doing all the work.

Sometimes the sub-conscious is busy even when you think you are fully aware of everything that is going on around. One particular time I remember cycling through Edinburgh and approaching a junction. Even though I wasn't aware of any danger, something in my head was screaming at me to stop. I listened, and stopped, just as a car pulled straight out of the junction at speed without looking. The driver saw me standing at the edge of the junction, realised she'd driven straight out into a busy road and slammed on her brakes...way too late. If I'd kept going, I'd have been squashed. My sub-conscious must have noticed the car not slowing down. It's easy to see how some people could attribute such an event to a higher god or benevolent being.

The rain started. I pulled on my already damp waterproofs as Al caught up. "This is shit" he grumbled, examining his tyres. They

191

were covered in grit but otherwise holding up. "I think it should get easier from here" I pointed to our position on the map. "It should be a slight downhill from here on I think".

We made our way along the edge of some small but long lochans. We were now making our way slowly through Bealach nam Meirleach which translates as 'Thief's pass'. Allegedly, people returning to the north after selling their goods were often ambushed here. Looking at a map it's easy to see why this pass was chosen as an ambush point, the hills for miles around are high and remote, with no other obvious routes through. The only possible low level route was to squeeze through this pass.

Even though the rain was continuing and we were still moving along, albeit at a slower pace than we'd have liked, the midges got noticeably worse as we reached the far end of the pass. They started to get properly annoying at just about the point the road surface started deteriorating. The bed rock was made of some kind of thin, slick, layers which protruded up out of the road surface. It suddenly became much more difficult to maintain forward momentum. Full concentration was now needed to navigate my bike over the bumps. It must have been worse for Al, but he was only a short way behind. This wasn't the enjoyable off tarmac jaunt through the hills we'd hoped it would be. It was rapidly becoming nightmarish. We struggled on another few kilometres until we turned a corner and the track headed down. For the next three kilometres we sped up and the midges didn't get a chance to congregate. Finally we reached Gobernuisgach Lodge, a fancy looking base for the shooting estate. Parked outside were several shiny 4x4s as well as a couple of beaten up old landrovers. We passed by. The road improved significantly.

We stopped to take a look at the map. This time we were joined by horseflies. Also known as 'clegs', these may not be a numerous as the swarming midge, but in comparison they are huge, and inflict a painful bite. "Shit!......evil..... little.......bastards....", I waved my arms around before hurriedly cycling off, leaving Al running around while trying to fold the map. From previous experience these things not only suck your blood, they cut your skin as they depart, leaving an itch that lasts a week. I wasn't hanging around.

It was only another couple of kilometres to the tarmac, which we reached after a steep climb. Not stopping for long on account of the beasties, we headed along the remotest of roads. It was now getting dark. We'd taken a lot longer than planned to cover the twelve kilometres of track road. It was time to use lights again, and hope that my batteries had enough left for the remaining distance.

The road, although tarmac, was so quiet it had a central strip of moss and vegetation which was holding on in the space between vehicle tyre tracks. We were now passing through a vast heathland, with only the odd roofless ruin of a house sitting in a patch of green, breaking the monotonous brown. We could see for miles all around. There wasn't another soul here. It was a little eerie as the drizzle continued and the light faded. Only the spinning of wheels, and clicking of ratcheted gears made any sound. I'm not sure about Al, but I was tired. And hungry. We hadn't eaten anything since an early lunch, some fifty kilometres, and an eternity, earlier.

We cycled on for twelve more kilometres in complete silence. Eventually, below us, appeared the lights of a village. Keeping an eye out for a decent spot to camp, we found one at a large lay-by, overlooking the lights below. It looked good. A nice flat grassy spot to sleep on. I suggested we could have set the tents up and then cycle the short distance down to the pub for some food. Al disagreed, he wanted to just go down to the village and find somewhere to camp later. We were both feeling a bit grumpy and had a discussion about it. Al won, mostly by just cycling off down the hill to the village of Altnaharra. Checkmate!....a winning move. I was forced to grumpily follow.

The village has a Met Office weather station and is mostly famous as the place which, each year, is mentioned in the news with headlines such as "Snow bound for three weeks in Britain's coldest village". In fact the lowest recorded temperature in Britain was measured here in 1995 at -27.5 degrees Centigrade. More importantly for us, it had a hotel and pub. Which surprisingly Al cycled straight past.

"I thought we were getting food before they stop serving?"

"No, we're going to find somewhere to camp" he replied.

Just the other side of the village we came to a wood which looked promising. A little explore away from the road and we found a good spot where we set up for the night. I ate some snacks while cooking up some pasta and immediately felt my mood improving. Soon enough we were talking again, and full of hot food. We walked back down the road to the hotel. Maybe it was the state of us, maybe the hotel was dead, but we were ushered into a tiny back room with a bar. Not really the fancy comfort I'd been expecting. Nonetheless they had some nice beers, of which we had a couple while chatting between ourselves and to the bar staff. We followed this with a whisky before heading back out into the cold night.

Day 6

The next morning I awoke to the sounds of machinery cutting wood in a nearby sawmill. I opened the tent door to let some fresh air in. No amazing views to be had here in the woods. The weather looked promisingly bright though, blue skies were overhead.

Today was our last day of cycling. We planned to head south to Lairg, only thirty-five kilometres away, where we'd catch a train back to normality. We got up and were welcomed to the new day by a large squadron of midges. An awful way to get up. 'probably if we'd stayed at the lay-by as I'd suggested we'd have been fine', I thought to myself. "Let's get out of here, get breakfast down the road?" Al agreed, and soon I was running around the wood while folding tent poles away and trying to keep the cloud of midges behind me. In record time I was packed, no need to be tidy today, the next time I'd be unpacking would be at home. A quick jog and push through the woods and we were free.

Three kilometres later, and up a long hill, we stopped next to some large flat rocks by the side of the road. The view behind was pretty good. We could see down and along Loch Naver and across to Ben Klibreck shaped like a whale, rising above the miles of relatively flat moorland surrounding it. The Ben is the second most northerly Munro at 962m high.

I sat on the rocks and constructed a chorizo and cheese sandwich breakfast while some coffee was brewing. The air was thankfully free of flying beasties. In was a very pleasant place to stop.

Refreshed, woken up, and reinvigorated, we took our time to get going. It was still early so we felt no need to rush.

We tackled the final few kilometres of the hill through desolate moorland. Our world was empty of other people and wildlife. No cars. No birds in the sky. Just us, rolling long. After

195

almost six kilometres of gentle uphill it finally flattened out for a distance before we rolled down to 'Crask Inn', known as the most remote pub in Britain, although I'm not convinced this is true. To my regret we didn't go in, we didn't feel ready to stop yet and cycled straight by. Apparently it has a huge range of whisky and beer. At any rate, it was still too early in the morning to partake of anything alcoholic.

The road continued for as far as I could see, completely flat. Now we were far from the mountains, the uninterrupted views were vast. We pushed on for final the twenty kilometres to Lairg, sitting at the south end of Loch Shin.

This was where our journey was to end. Or nearly. We found the station, due to the local geography, was actually three kilometres out of town, further down the main road. Once there, the timetables showed that a train wasn't due for another couple of hours. Pondering whether there was anything in Lairg to occupy us, we came to the conclusion that as the railway line more or less followed the route of the road and as there were other stations, we may as well just keep cycling.

So, this we did. The map showed a nicer, smaller parallel road going down the far side of the valley with 'Shin Falls' visitor centre marked some distance down the road. Unfortunately, the road started back in Lairg. There was, however, a dotted line marked on the map, leading from the station across a bridge and connecting to the more interesting road. It took us a few minutes of scooting around to find the start of the path. At first it was perfectly cyclable, but quickly it headed steeply down with steps. We were forced to carry our bikes the last section to the river before crossing. It was worth the trouble though, the road was much quieter.

We stopped to look at Shin Falls and have an expensive cup of tea at the café (which has since been demolished after a fire). It was strange to find the small shop, in the middle of nowhere, was branch of Harrods! "Maybe you should go in and get yourself a designer bag?" I suggested to Al. He replied with a derision conveying snort. On looking it up right now while writing this, it appears the owner of Harrods also owns the estate containing the falls, which makes it less strange.

We sat at a table outside to keep an eye on the bikes. Soon, some flying insects appeared to disturb our break. This time wasps. At first a single wasp flitted about the remains of some sugary food left on the table. Before long it was joined by others. It was probably time to get going.

Before long, the nice road ran out, and we were back on the main one. To the side of the road, on the side of a wooded hill, was a huge castle. Built by the Duchess of Sutherland in 1917, the grand building was the result of a settlement between the Duchess and the Sutherland family after they were unhappy at her choice of marriage partner. She was given the funds to build her own castle as long as it was outside of Sutherland. So she choose to build it right on the edge of the region, on a raised hill, visible to a large part of Sutherland and right next to the main road and rail routes south. For this, it became known as the 'Castle of spite'. If it were my castle, I'm not sure how much spite I'd be able to muster towards those who paid for it, but the Duchess obviously had her reasons. She also ensured that the clock tower had a clock face on each side except for the north side which could be seen from Sutherland. Allegedly, this was because she "wouldn't give them the time".

The castle was bought by Colonel Salevsen, a wealthy business man, who allowed it to be used as a safe retreat by the King and Prince of Norway during the Nazi occupation. Eventually, in 1945, the Colonel's son, who'd inherited the castle, gave the castle and its contents to the Scottish Youth Hostel Association. It remained probably one of the most amazing Youth Hostels in the world until recently when, like all good things, they were forced by huge repair bills (they spent two million trying to keep the castle) to sell it to developers who'll no doubt turn it into a luxury hotel.

We arrived at Invershin Station. Given we still had time until the train, and we were enjoying the ride, we decided to keep cycling and re-evaluate at the next station. We knew we were getting towards the end and raced down the road. There was a terrible headwind which made it doubly hard going but five kilometres and a short time later we arrived at Bonar Bridge. I was sweating profusely after going as hard as I could. Al got off his bike and lay on a wall breathing heavily. "I need some sugar" I said, and headed to a shop to get some coke. I sat on the wall enjoying it as Al reappeared from the shop eating an ice cream. I think we were finally done.

We cycled the last kilometre across the flat head of the Dornoch Firth estuary to reach the village of Ardgay and the train station. We checked the timetable; thirty minutes until the train. We needed to be on the platform at the opposite side of the tracks and so with weary legs we lifted our bikes and carried them up and over the old iron Victorian pedestrian bridge. Al set up his stove and started making some coffee. I went for a walk. It was very short, there was really nothing here. I stopped to have a look a large quartz white rock sitting next to the station entrance with an intriguing looking plaque in front. Turns out that this is the "Clach Eiteag", a stone which was moved from town to town to mark the position of the next local market. Thing is, the stone was massive. God knows this thing was moved around.

I returned to the station and a cup of hot coffee. I finished just as the train pulled in.

Mountain Bike Orienteering

I arrived at the race start point, Selkirk rugby club, in the pouring rain on a mean, cold morning. Driving past the tents of the folks who'd stayed over from the mountain bike marathon the day before, I wondered how many of them would be taking part in the orienteering race given the weather and their probable tired legs. I parked up, and after registering, got my bike ready in the already busy area under the gazebo.

Participants in these races have to carry an electronic timing tag which monitors their race. Small electronic stations are placed at the start/finish as well as checkpoints around the course. A racer's progress is monitored when they push their wrist tag into a hole in the electronic station. A reassuring 'beep' sounds, and the current time and checkpoint number are recorded by the tag. At the end of a race the data from the tags are downloaded onto a laptop. This allows the organisers to calculate completions, performance and most importantly points.

I was early, hardly anyone else was here. I procrastinated for a while, chatting to the few others who had so far turned up, and continued to fiddle with the sticky brake that had troubled me on a previous ride. Really, I was just waiting for the rain to stop.
        However, much as I willed the weather gods to intervene, it was becoming clear it wasn't going to get better any time soon. It was time to go.

I started my stopwatch and 'dibbed' my electronic tag into the start control. I now had three hours to gather as many points from checkpoints arranged around the course as I could. It's not just a simple case of reaching as many checkpoints as possible, they are also worth different values, depending both on distance to reach them, and the difficulty involved (e.g. how big a hill they are

199

positioned on top of).

I was handed a map and, after clipping it into my map-board, chasing after my dropped checkpoint list (which provides short descriptions of where the electronic checkpoints are such as "bench at viewpoint"), knocking a bulldog clip off of someone else's map board while moving in the cramped space under the gazebo, finding and re-attaching it, I was ready to go......almost. Depending on the race, you usually don't get to see where the checkpoints are before your timer has started, making route planning a hurried affair and an integral part of the race. I spent a few precious minutes quickly working out an initial route.

I decided to go up the big hills first so after set off straight to checkpoint 12 at the bottom of a track road for an easy ten points. It's always good for confidence to get something in the bag quickly. From here I had a choice to make; up the steep hill to the east and along a path marked as "indistinct/boggy", or along the gently climbing track road straight to a 25 pointer above a waterfall. Hmmm...I went for the latter, and after a short walk through some spiky bushes to find the control, I continued up the main track, ignoring the alternative route straight up to checkpoint 9 as it looked too steep, indistinct and slow. Instead I decided to stick to the main track for several long kilometres, picking up a couple more checkpoints along the way before detouring up a very steep path to the right. The path started out alright, but as I pushed hard on the pedals, slowly climbing higher, the path became more and more waterlogged until I found myself cycling up a fast flowing river. The rushing water was forming deep ruts in the gravel path and small rocks were washing down at speed and pinging off of my wheels as they passed. I stopped to register my electronic 'dibber' at the checkpoint attached to a gate across the path. By now I was soaked through, my gloved hands were cold and my shoes were full of water.

I was now on the final climb to the top. I thought it couldn't be far. I pushed on, peering through the thick mist, waiting for the three huge stone markers I knew were positioned on the very top of the hill, to appear. After a hard climb I finally saw the summit and after not quite making it up the last steep kick-up without getting off and pushing, I grabbed the scant five points available. I stopped for a minute to work out an onwards route.

One of the aspects I like about bike orienteering is that although fitness plays a big part, it's a bit more cerebral that other bike races. Good map reading skills are important, as is route strategy. Attacking a route in the 'wrong' direction can be catastrophic as you find yourself dragging your bike up a steep hill you hadn't noticed on the map. I learnt early on that taking a much longer track road to reach a certain point is often quicker and less energy sapping than taking a short cut. Sometimes taking a risky looking track can pay off, often you'll find yourself up to your knees in mud wishing for a quick death.

From my current position, there were two obvious paths down from the ridge of the hill, both of which headed in different directions and both of which had high value checkpoints strung along them. I decided to try for both, which meant climbing back up the hill twice!

The first bit of single-track was awesome. A fun path down straight down through the forest with a steep, twisty section at the end. I slid my way down at speed, back wheel locking up around the tightest of the corners. I love these fast flowy bits of mountain biking.

After climbing back up the track road, my legs were burning. When I reached the final junction and saw how steep the last road to the top was, I thought 'nope' and instead continued on to join the second bit of single track lower down, missing out the top fifteen points.

I gave it a good go but the first section down the hill was un-rideable. A rooty mud slurry. I gave up and pushed through the forest, dibbing my tracker token a couple of times along the way.

The last section looked better, I splashed through the first couple of puddles. I hit the third one and my front wheel disappeared into a deep, bike eating hole. I teetered forwards, the event unfolding in slow motion, somehow giving me time to think 'aww bollocks!' and feeling a heart stopping tension followed by surge of adrenaline before, somehow, not quite going over the handlebars.

The lowest control collected, I settled in for the long climb back to the top. Someone passed me going in the other direction. I'm not sure who. I was just glad to see I wasn't alone out here.

Once I reached the top, I dipped back into the forest and out again to collect the fifteen points I'd missed earlier. Then continued along the ridge, picking up the final hilltop points, hoicking my bike over a wall, and then happily heading back down towards the bottom of the valley, passing a friend who was going the other way, and picking up a huge fifty points on the way.

I could see on the map a medium value checkpoint in a wood on the opposite side of the valley. After making my way across, I slid my way down a very muddy trail between the trees. Almost falling off a couple of times, and going frustratingly slowly, I gave up and pushed. Once I finally reached the checkpoint I could see a track road not far away. Rather that retrace my route through the mud, I cut through the forest to the track, lifting my bike over branches and jumping over ditches.

The next checkpoints were picked up along the relatively easy to cycle paths which run along Yarrow Water back towards Selkirk. I joined the main road for a section where I shouted "different race!" at the wildly gesticulating marshal who tried to direct me down a side road.

Picking up two more checkpoints I checked my rapidly disintegrating map. What I'd initially thought was a bridge, was just a weir. This screwed up my planned route. Not only that, but I was now forced to cycle into the fully dissolved hole in my map. I got lucky. I knew checkpoint 17 ("large drainage dome") was around here somewhere, but I wasn't even sure what side of the river it was on. I also didn't know if the path I was on joined back anywhere useful.

Things worked out on both counts. I couldn't miss the huge dome when I came across it, and the path ended right next to the start point at the rugby club.

I checked my watch. Due to my screw-up with the non-bridge, I had twenty minutes left! Looking at the map I saw a twenty-five pointer. It was a long way, but it was tarmac all the way.

Another aspect of bike orienteering was now coming into play. Unlike other races, you have no-idea how the other competitors are doing. You don't start at the same time and you usually take different routes. When you see another rider out on the course, you've no idea if they started before or after you. You don't know if they've had time to collect that checkpoint you missed out. If you do happen to cycle along together for a bit, you have nothing to compare yourself with except their current speed. When it comes to the end of the race it's hard to know whether to attempt to reach a risky extra checkpoint or not. If you return to the finish after the race time, you are penalised for every minute on an exponential scale. You have to calculate whether the value of the checkpoint is worth being late for. I've felt great during a race, thinking things have gone well, which means not getting lost, or making bad route choices, only to find myself way down in the points table. Conversely, I've spent races staring at my map, digging around in the undergrowth looking for a non-existent checkpoint, slowly becoming demoralised. Only to find once I'd returned that everyone else had the same issues and I'd done quite well.

In this race, I decided to give the last checkpoint ten minutes and, if I was no-where close, turn back. The one-way roads through Selkirk wasted a few minutes but then I was on the long pedal back into the countryside. The control was at the top of another steep climb (of course it was!). This was where, almost exactly a year ago, I'd crashed and broke my knee!

My knee was certainly reminding me of this now. I turned around, carefully descended the steep section, and then floored it back the way I'd come. I somehow found enough energy to overtake a couple of people doing the road ride. I cut the corners as I raced down the last hill back through Selkirk, cut through an open gate into the side of the rugby club and raced for the finish.

I slid to a stop next to the finish control and fumbled about trying to get my wrist tag to register. Finally, "beeeeeep", and I could relax. I thought I was late, but wasn't sure by how much. The first few minutes are worth a few points each but after that you start to lose a serious amount. The difference between registering 5:59 and 6 minutes can make all the difference.
I soon found out I'd made it back only 2 minutes late, which only equated to me losing 3 points.

After quickly changing out of my sodden clothes, I headed in to warm up with some of the excellent home-made carrot, ginger and butter-nut squash soup followed by cakes.

The results calculated, I found out I was equal in collected points with the consistently unbeatable Jonathan. However, he'd come in a minute later than me, meaning I'd somehow scraped first place by a single point. Despite the weather, possibly because of it, it was lots of fun.

Gravel Race

As this book is about cycling adventures in Scotland, and as the start point of this small adventure, Kielder, is actually a couple of kilometres on the wrong side of the Scottish border it did cross my mind that maybe it shouldn't be included. But then, it's a good story and I'm writing this, and who cares anyway, and do we even really exist? Regardless, the route taken does cross the border into Scotland for a while. The landscape, people and sights remained the same. The only things to change were the laws. Did you know that in Scotland it's illegal for a boy under the age of 10 to see a naked mannequin? If you want to indulge in that kind of perversion, then in Kielder you can feel free to indulge. Although, when crossing the border, make sure to leave your Polish potatoes behind as since 2004 it's illegal to import them into England.

I did once do another cross-border cycle orienteering event, very near to Kielder in fact, where the rules changed depending on which side of the border we were currently on. On the north side, we were allowed to ride anywhere within reason, on the south, only roads and bridleways. We weren't permitted to use footpaths, tracks unmarked on the map, or cut across the countryside.

I can't remember where I first heard about the Kielder 200, but I do remember I was immediately interested. Billed as a gravel endurance event rather than a mountain bike race it sounded like something a bit different to what I'd tried before. I signed up and through the ever present Facebook discovered that a couple of friends, had also signed up.

I hadn't heard of any similar events in the UK and indeed this turned out to be one of the first of its kind. Gravel racing was already popular in the USA where there are something like 1.3 million miles of quiet non-tarmac roads to race on. The event routes are always on unpaved roads and tracks, and the riding is always fast paced. However, the track surfaces can range from hard packed smooth and fast, to rough, rutted and muddy. So from one kilometre to the next the riding can change from easy rolling, to a bike carrying nightmare.

The ideal bike for these races is a modified cyclocross bike. These look like normal road bikes with their thin wheels and curved drop handlebars. The main differences being they are built to be tougher, are geared more for hills, and have voluminous tyres with better grip patterns to cope with the rough terrain. These bikes are generally faster on track roads and lighter than mountain bikes.

I don't have a gravel/cyclocross bike. So for this event I'd be using my normal hard-tail mountain bike. Knowing the route was two-hundred kilometres long I decided I'd need to get some long rides in beforehand and set about getting a few months of weekends riding the longer, tougher routes I knew. As I learned more about the event, I began to wonder what I'd let myself in for. I started to become a bit more concerned about being able to make the distance. Two weeks before the event, the organisers released a map and GPS file. I downloaded the file and examined the route it to find that it was slightly short of two-hundred kilometres, coming in at 195km. Well that was the good news. The bad news was that it showed 3700 metres of climbing. So only four Munro's (the largest hills in Scotland) worth. Or over twice the height climbed by the Tour De France when the route takes them up Mont Ventoux.

As if this wasn't enough, the organisers had also set time limits for reaching certain points: five hours to reach the first checkpoint at 60km, and ten hours to reach the 130km checkpoint. This meant that to get past the second checkpoint I'd have to average 13km/hour which actually didn't sound too bad until you start factoring in any stops for mechanicals, food and so on. All of which would only push the required riding speed upwards.

I was now feeling slightly intimidated by the distance, the amount of hills to be climbed and even the possible tedium of cycling so far on track roads. My aim was just to be able to finish. I wanted one of the woven badges handed out to anyone who made the distance. I set about making the last couple of weeks before the event count.

I made a couple of changes to my bike to help cope with the

distance. First I shortened an old set of handlebars I had spare, and stuck some nineties' bar-ends on. I wouldn't be needing the leverage provided by wide bars as the terrain shouldn't be too difficult. The alternative grip options provided by adding bar ends would hopefully ease the numbness and pain in my hands and arms I've felt on other long distance events. I also added two water bottles and cages. Usually I prefer to keep the bike itself light and manoeuvrable, and carry water in a backpack bladder, but for cycling long distances it's better to not have the weight of all that water on your back. The weekend before the event I decided to go for a very long ride as some sort of late preparation. Most of the day I pedalled, deliberately modifying the route to take in as many hills as I could. The tracks and paths were fast and dry and although I hoped these were tougher surfaces and steeper hills than anything I'd be seeing in the event, I was surprised to find that at the end of the day I'd ridden 84km. Less than half the required distance. I'd also only climbed a total of 1,600 metres. Worse still, I was completely exhausted. This didn't bode well.

I left work early and drove for a couple of hours to Kielder camp-site where I'd be staying the night. I forgot how great the second half of the journey was. I weaved my way along tiny single lane roads, passing remote farms and small hamlets. All the while not meeting a single other car. It was already beginning to feel remote.

Eventually, I arrived at the camp-site and set up my tent on the least muddy area I could find....which was still quite muddy. My neighbours made the mistake of driving their van onto the grass, whereupon it quickly stuck, wheels spinning, flinging mud comically around. I helped to push, but it was going nowhere. Sticking a large rock under one of the front wheels was the solution and the, now not so white, van was soon free.

I talked with another camper who had arrived at the site on his bike and carrying a large backpack.
"Did you cycle far?"
"Yeah, from Hexham. The bloody bus refused to carry my bike."
"How far is that?"

"Oohhh...let see...about 60km, partly off-road. Not the ideal start for tomorrow."

No. No it wasn't.

I registered, got my race pack and went to bed early, resisting the offer of going to the pub presented by another camper.

I didn't get the best night's sleep. It was bloody freezing. I was also excited about the race and knowing I'd have to wake up early always means I sleep badly. After hours of fitful snoozing my alarm went off at 6am and I wearily climbed out of my sleeping bag. I was surprised on opening the tent door to find a thin layer of snow covering the ground. At least the mud was now frozen.

Some granola and a pot of coffee later, it was time to go. I feel excited and nervous as I ride up the hill to the start point at Kielder Castle. I find several hundred other cyclists hanging around as they discuss their choices of bikes, tyres and food. I couldn't see any of the few people I knew, so just joined the crowd as we jostled our way forwards into some kind of start formation. A race briefing was being shouted out to the front of the crowd. I couldn't hear a word. Later a marshal paraphrased the announcement for those of us who didn't hear; "don't be an arse, and don't die!" The world suddenly became much brighter. The first sliver of the sun appeared from behind a hill, as if controlled precisely by the challenge organisers. And then, with a wave of a marshal's arms, the first bunch of riders were off.

The race timing was being done by tags attached to lanyards which we'd 'dib' into an electronic checkpoint as we passed. So, it didn't matter how far back in the stream of cyclists you actually passed the start point. It all worked out fairly in the end. Anyway, there were a few kilometres of warm up before the first checkpoint.

Finally, it was my turn to go. I headed off, glad to be at last pedalling. A chance to warm up. I was soon through the first checkpoint, with a 'good luck!' from the marshal. My personal timer was now running. Immediately we hit the first hill. People were bunched together, filling the width of the track. I was determined that in order to survive the distance I needed to go at my own pace. Plenty of people were faster, sprinting off up the hill, but plenty of people were slower too. I weaved my way through the crowd, catching the back wheel of faster riders when I could in order to ease my passage forwards. Soon, the riders spread out and I could relax into my own pedalling rhythm.

The first part of the ride to the 60km checkpoint was fairly uneventful, although a fairly long section off of the 'easy' track roads and into a thick, overgrown, forest track with ruts filled with mud and slippery rocks, was unexpected. I was already thinking about food. I knew that even at the early point I should be eating something every half an hour or so. But it was just too early in the morning. I didn't feel like eating. Even so, after an hour and a half I reached into a pocket on my backpack and pulled out an oat and honey bar I'd bought during the drive down. They looked like good cycling food. I popped one in my mouth. God, it was awful. Tasteless and dry......sooo dry! I wasn't going to eat any more of those horrible things. I reached back into the pocket and pulled out a Snickers. Not often I eat chocolate bars at 8.30 in the morning. But it did the job.

It was a beautiful day, the low spring sun was bright and although there was a chillingly cold wind, it wasn't strong.

I reached the first checkpoint, made sure to remember to 'dib' my timing lanyard, and helped myself to malt loaf and a banana. A quick refill of my water bottles and ten minutes after arriving I was off again.

The next section I started to feel the first hints of pain. I'm not used to just sitting on a saddle and spinning my legs like a road biker. During my mountain bike miles, I'm forced by the terrain and the constant search for traction to be constantly changing position on the bike, shifting my weight around and moving around on the saddle. Pedalling cadence also changes with the surface type and gradient. Instead here I was, spending a long time sitting in the exact same position. My lower back and bum were beginning to ache.

I turned a corner to see a deep river crossing ahead. People were sitting at either side. Evidently, many had decided to remove shoes and socks to keep them dry while wading across. Someone sped past and made it most of the way across before putting their feet down. They didn't topple over, but it looked like a close thing. Me, I just waded through without bothering to remove my shoes. I couldn't be bothered with the rigmarole of getting changed. It was cold.

I chatted with someone going the same speed as we rode along. "I'm a bit sick of the view now" he said. We'd so far mostly been in thick forest with nothing but uniform trees and the road ahead to look at. Just minutes later, we emerged out into the open hilltops. The view took my mind off the grind. Next came a long downhill section over very rough terrain. I sped down the hill, standing on the pedals, hopping over dips in the road and weaving down the best line. I was suddenly really enjoying myself. The downhill seemed endless although it was probably only ten minutes of fun.

Before I knew it I'd reached the second food stop at 100km. I was feeling tired now. I stayed a while, eating some proper food (sandwiches) and warming my cold feet on a fire-pit beneath an open tepee. I was thinking about leaving when a sudden hail shower started. "Maybe just another few minutes by the fire" I thought to myself. Before I'd managed to finish another piece of chocolate brownie, the sun reappeared and the hail stopped.

We crossed the border into Scotland and rode past Newcastleton. I'd remembered looking at this part of the course on my computer beforehand and thinking "the track looks like it just follows the river for miles slowly rising. It's going to be an easy bit".

I was wrong. The gradient was fine, the problem was that the road surface was terrible. The sizes of the rocks, and the spaces in-between, created an energy sapping vibration. Legs had to work hard just to keep the bike moving. And every bump was felt in my back and bum. I was glad I was on a mountain bike for this section, it would have been even more brutal with smaller tyres. I was glad to have some company along this section. I chatted with another mountain biker as we endured the torment. It went on for a long time, until finally, just when the surface began to improve, we were directed onto the biggest, steepest climb of the day. It was here I started to have stomach cramps, just to add to my woes. The climbs were endless. I started to wonder whether I was going to make it, eventually concluding that as long as my stomach didn't get any worse I'd probably survive. Now my back was really aching. I switched gears and although it's not an efficient way to climb, I stood up for a bit pumping the pedals and stretching, which gave some short term relief.

After the huge climbs came some amazing descents. Long, smooth tracks led for kilometres along the valleys. I was barely pedalling yet reaching speeds of over 40km/h for long periods. It was brilliant. By the time I reached the last food stop, I was feeling much better and thinking the last 50km should be one of the easiest sections.

Refuelled and only slightly rested, I set off, happy in the knowledge that, mechanical issues aside, I was probably going to finish. Unfortunately, it soon became clear the pain wasn't going to end yet. The route took me up a leg bursting 6km long climb. I decided it was time to deploy a morale booster. I dug some earphones out of a pocket, stuck them into my phone and put on some loud music.

I flew down the other side, turned a sharp corner and was directed onto the smooth, twisty, undulating, wonderful path which looped around the picturesque Kielder water. I was now less than 25k from the finish. The remaining section was fast and fun. I was passed by lots of people zooming past on their cx bikes. But it didn't matter. I was nearly there. I passed a sign that marked 10km to go and then a detour from the GPS track meant there was a final steep but thankfully short hill to climb, before I was directed along the main road. Another hail shower started, heavier than before. As I struggled along into the wind, I watched the tiny white balls bouncing off of my front tyre.

Before I knew it, I was on the road leading up the finish point at the castle. I'd done it! I dibbed into the finish checkpoint and then had a chat with a marshal. "Are you happy?" he asked. Maybe I looked as tired as I felt. "Yeah, that was good!"

I rolled into the finish area, dumped my bike, and lay down on a bench. I found myself shivering uncontrollably. I had absolutely nothing left.

It was, I think, the hardest ride I've ever done. I'd somehow covered 195km and 3800m of climbing in 10hours and 35 minutes (including the stops). That was way faster than I'd ever imagined I could do. My average riding speed was just over 20km/h!

Would I do it again?.......Ask me in a couple of weeks.

By the same author:

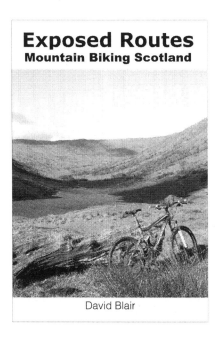

A mountain biking route guide book with some of the more spectacular, longer, and less well know routes in Scotland. As well as a couple of the best classics updated.

17 routes across Scotland, with detailed descriptions and annotated maps in an easy to carry format (102 pages).

Also provided are notes about the areas you are passing through, including some history and the wildlife you may be lucky enough to see.

Available from Amazon.co.uk and iworm.co.uk

Made in the USA
Middletown, DE
16 October 2017